THE DIRT

Family Life on an Iowa Farm—
Stories to Entertain and Inspire

By Karen Schwaller

Published by:
Karen Schwaller
Milford, Iowa 51351

ISBN-13: 978-1523229277
ISBN-10: 1523229276

Library of Congress Control Number: 2013944820

Second Printing January 2016

This book is lovingly dedicated to my family—

My husband, Dave, and our children, Emily, Doug and Dustin, who have given me so much to write about over the years.

Thank you for not minding when I wrote about our lives on the farm. You have given my life great purpose and meaning, and I love you all.

TABLE OF CONTENTS

THE DIRT

Family Life on an Iowa Farm—
Stories to Entertain and Inspire

CHOOSING HUSBANDS AND SEED CORN

For years, farmers have known the importance of selecting good seed and livestock, and caring for it.

They pass that valuable knowledge on to their growing children, hoping that someday it will be part of the legacy they leave behind when it becomes the responsibility of the next generation to feed the world.

But today I'm here to speak to that new generation of women who have not yet even met their farmer husbands-to-be. I'm talking about selecting and caring for just the right farmer husband, and I'm a-"maized" at how closely it parallels the plight of selecting the right seed corn. From the discovery of the unique specimen to the engagement period, there's a lot to consider. I learned this as my father showed me a seed corn salesman's manual—a little black book that told him everything there was to know about one particular brand of seed corn. Really, it sent chills down my stalk, and it still does.

The first section in the seed corn manual is called "Introduction." This is most important in selecting a husband. Without the introduction, we would all be old maids—or farm widows during more than just the arduous planting and harvesting seasons, or the relentless football season.

The next two sections are called "The Association" and "Hybrids." This would tell you all about the farmer's immediate and extended family, what kind of stock he came from and how he stacks up against others like him—most important for would-be wives to know in the event that there are some shifty-acting relatives who aren't even in front of a steering wheel.

Ironically, there are many categories in the "Husbandry" section of the seed corn manual itself, including the following:

*VARIETIES: Shopping around for a husband is important indeed. If your finalists on the list all happen to chew tobacco, it would be wise to choose the one who can spit it the furthest away from you.

*STALK HEIGHT: If it's important that your husband is taller than you, you'll want to pay special attention to this category.

*STANDING ABILITY: Have a fight just once and you'll find this out toot sweet. Of course, if you go shopping for clothing for extended periods of time and he stands around waiting while you're in the dressing room, you have a squabble AND you'll see if he can stand through a 30-minute ceremony. Efficiency is a wonderful thing.

*KERNEL INDENTATION: Check out the face. If the worry lines are deep, proceed with caution—he may be a worrywart. If the laugh lines are deep, don't ever let him watch you do your aerobics tape unless you have the right underwear to support everything that will be moving.

*DEPTH OF KERNEL: This one I take to mean his integrity or even his IQ. Your man will need his kernel pretty deep if he's gonna take on farming for a living, or your family—even your Uncle Vern, who returned a changed man following that incident with a barbed wire fence, a skunk and an icy patch.

*EAR LENGTH: Directionally proportional to how well he listens; or maybe he was just a kid who always showed up where the trouble was, and his dad pulled his ears a lot to get him to tell the truth.

The "General Comments" section also has good reference points, including:

*HEAVY, SOLID EARS: Always listening for the next item in the "Honey-Do List." An absolute **must** for women who dislike changing fuses or removing deceased household livestock from traps.

*ATTRACTIVE or SHOWY IN THE FIELD, or BOUNTIFUL APPEARANCE: Certainly a must for the wise husband shopper. You must see him as handsome as he commands the steering wheel of a tractor, wearing a flannel shirt, dirty blue jeans and greasy seed corn cap. And with his "bountiful appearance," you may think about packing an apple in his lunch instead of the usual cookie/snack cake combo.

*STRAIGHT KERNEL ROWS: You should know if he's crooked right from the start.

*EXCELLENT YIELDER: It's a little on the personal side, but if you want to have a family someday, this one is extremely important.

*EXPOSED EAR TIPS: Unless you want to marry Mr. Spock from the Starship Enterprise, this would hardly be an issue.

*WIDELY ADAPTED: If he can adapt to your family and your way of cleaning chickens, you'll see your 65th wedding anniversary.

*DROUGHT RESISTANT: This is extremely important to know. If he can hang with you even when things aren't going well and the well of passion is running dry, you'll have a keeper.

This column by Karen Schwaller first
appeared in *Farm News*.

A FARM WIFE'S WEDDING VOWS

The longer I share the same last name as a farmer, the more I realize that I'm actually a woman who has vowed to stay one step behind all the little animals . . . short of keeping a pooper-scooper handy in my hip pocket.

I'm talking about the fact that I could also write a book echoing author and football professional Gayle Sayers' piece called, "I Am Third." In his book he writes that God is first, his family is second, and he is third.

Mine would more accurately define the farm wife by reasoning that, "The farming comes first, a shower is second and I am third."

As most farm wives will tell you, those aromatic critters with four legs usually come first. Which is not to say that it offends me that a sheep with its head stuck in a fence should come before my own needs, or that equipment breakdowns at strategic times of the year can lead to days of meeting each other coming and going, leaving little time for idle chatter.

It's just that wedding terminology and the excitement of the wedding day conveniently hide these basic farm facts of life.

Therefore, I have compiled my own set of wedding vows for every farm wife on her wedding day, throwing those old, traditional vows out to pasture. After all, in these days of prenuptial agreements and push-button and online relationships, we who would marry a farmer have a right to know exactly what we're getting into.

You know those traditional vows—"To have and to hold, from this day forward, in good times and in bad, in sickness and in health, for richer for poorer, for better for worse, till death do us part."

Pretty gutsy thing to agree to, if I do say so myself. Gives me shivers just thinking about it.

Mine go like this: "To feed and maintain, from this day through forward contracting and the futures, in times when farming goes smoothly and when elements make it seem unbearable, through mystery swine disease and critical livestock health, through steak-for-dinner years and hot dogs-for-dinner years, from farming with new green equipment to farming with a dinosaur Allis Chalmers tractor, till the rendering truck makes its final call."

Those embarking on marriage and life on the farm should be entitled to a whole different set of vows, since the days of stopping at dark, and quality vs. quantity time went out with the concept of actually walking beans. Everything is getting bigger, and it takes more time and more money.

My own mother, married to a farmer for fifty-four years in all, has said that the farming and livestock usually came before the things that needed to be done in the house by a pair of hands that knew their way around the back panels and insides of appliances. And I know she wasn't alone.

A friend of mine once told me that her mother had endured the same syndrome during the years they've had cattle. She smiled as she told me her advice to her mother, "I said, 'Mother, you need to grow a tail, and then you might get more attention.'"

And yet, here we are, farm wives ready on a moment's notice to help feed, chase, sort, load, move and haul livestock, clean farrowing crates, drive a tractor, put up hay, and a list of other chores that also don't seem very feminine. We live our lives beside the men we have promised ourselves to, because we, too, have grown to tolerate—and then enjoy—farm life.

So farm wives and farm-wives-to-be, take heart. You may not always come first, but just think of how you would look with a tail.

This column by Karen Schwaller first
appeared in *Farm News*.

BEWARE THE FARMER'S PLIERS

There's just something about the relationship a farmer holds with his pair of pliers . . . and don't tell me you haven't noticed it.

They do more bonding than Elmer's glue if they have a pliers in their side holder. After all, it's one of the first things they pick up when they get ready for the day—on goes the belt, on goes the pliers holder, then the jeans pockets get stuffed with everything a family of six would need for a two-year wilderness survival test.

If your farmer husband had some dehydrated daily rations to occupy space in his pockets, you'd probably never see him again.

And maybe being best pals with a pair of pliers isn't the worst thing in the world. After all, a farmer and his pliers are together more than he is with his family, and unlike strange cousin "Whatshisname," they're always right beside him to offer a helping hand, no matter what the circumstances . . . from fixing a fence to scraping dried-on feed from out of a feeder, to spreading it through the hog you-know-what to finding a nail that fell into it, to using it as a clamp with which to carry dead livestock out of the farrowing house. There was never a more all-purpose handyman's tool.

And it seems no matter what the farmer's mood, he's never unhappy to see his faithful pair of pliers. If they've been lost— even for a few minutes—it's comparable in nature to a restaurant running out of food. It renders him completely vulnerable and useless . . . and in somewhat of a panic.

"What's the matter?" I once asked my husband, seeing the exasperation in his face after we had finished chasing some hogs.

6

"Oh, I lost my (#$%^*!) pliers!" he retorted. "Can you help me look for 'em?"

I wondered if he would be that upset if he found that I had one day disappeared after we chased hogs.

It still could happen, the way things go out in the yards sometimes.

I don't mind helping him, but there is a limit to my good-heartedness, ya know? Sometimes when we're working on something, he'll hand me his pliers if he thinks I need them. To me, it's worth a five-minute trip to the house to get my handy household pliers, which have seen nothing but appliances and the edges of mouse traps with dead mice dangling from them.

I'll usually gladly accept his cordial sharing of his pliers—if I have my work gloves on to shield me from all the things I know are living and probably producing families on the handles.

Farm wives ought not be jealous of the allegiance their husbands feel toward their pliers. After all, if those pliers are the only things they pick up regularly during all those years together, then perhaps we ought to feel lucky in this modern age of disposable marriages . . .

That also reminds me that my husband has a pair of insulated overalls which need the pliers pocket fixed before that awful white stuff comes falling out of the skies. If the pocket doesn't get fixed and the pliers get lost, I know which one of us (the coveralls or me) will get tossed out the door first into the nearest snow bank.

If six-shooters were an old-time cowboy's line of defense against the perils of his occupation, then today the same would hold true about a pair of pliers for a modern-day farmer . . . even one who isn't so modern. Probably *especially* farmers who are not so modern because they have to fix and fix and fix instead of buying new things to replace things that have broken.

That tells you what kind of farming operation we have had here at the Schwallers'.

Still, a farm wife must know that an extra pair or two of pliers stashed away can take the sting out of the moment her husband loses track of his. Although it is undoubtedly not the same broken-in pair he has lost, it certainly is better than listening to him eulogize his lost appendage for the following half hour.

Perhaps a little advice might be to put one in his Christmas stocking so he can bond with it before he actually needs it, eliminating that awkward, breaking-in period.

It just might put you a couple of points closer to that old faithful pair of pliers in your husband's popularity ratings.

This column by Karen Schwaller first appeared
in the *Sioux City Journal.*

BIRTHING THE CALF

It was one of those days that is so typical on the farm. I had somewhere to be, and since all of our guys were out running field cultivators, anhydrous tanks and oat seeders, it was my job to check the sheep and cows before I left to see if there were any impending babies.

I had decided earlier that as long as I didn't have to check *myself* for impending babies before I left, that I was still ahead of the game.

You know you're a farm wife when you don't think anything of running around behind farm animals to look at their behinds to see if anything is hanging out of there. While in the past I have felt a little like a well-meaning pervert as I've checked pregnant farm animals, I'm amazed at how "high-brow" societal norms are for humans under the same circumstances. There are only a select group of women I know who would be okay with people coming around to see if some part of them is hanging out behind them.

Not expecting anything much out in the yards since there had been quite a lull in the action for a couple of weeks, I slipped on my "you-know-what"-kickers and headed toward the sheep barn. Nothing going on there, so it was out to the lady bovines, which were looking quite pristine as they stood around chewing their cud, looking at me and waiting to be moms.

A glance from the 50-yard-line didn't show any new calves anywhere, but a view from a more up close and personal angle told a different story.

I got around behind this particular cow, and of course—since there had been no calves born for a couple of weeks, and now I needed to be somewhere in 40 minutes—I saw a calf hoof out in plain view. It was a classic case of "Murphy's Law of the Farm" if I ever saw one—nothing happens until you're ready to go somewhere.

So—I dialed up "1-800-Husband" to see if there were any specific instructions. I've seen many pigs and sheep be born, but never a calf—even at my age.

One of our sons came home and took over the mid-wife role. I was officially relieved of that duty. Had I been the one to do this myself, my relief would probably have taken a much different form . . . especially thinking about possible complications as the process went on.

We got the cow into the barn and let her settle down, while our son and I chatted quietly in the next room, peering through an opening between the gate and the wall so we could watch her.

Our son was tallying up the number of calves they had with this one, and was doing the financial math, dreaming of what could someday be for him and his brother. It's fun when your kids tell you their dreams.

The cow was only about half settled about 20-30 minutes into it when our son said he had a lot of other things to get done that day, and decided he was "going in." It was pretty official—he grabbed the O.B. sleeves and some twine string. I would have grabbed the safety goggles, hip waders, rubber gloves and saran wrap and covered my entire body.

You never know.

We then penned her up in a smaller area so we could get her into the chute. She was like a super-sized bagel trying to fit into a bread-sized toaster slot.

"Oh, poor mama," I thought. I began to feel compassion toward this beast. She and I could have something in common—there have been plenty of times when I didn't fit in, too.

Going with what we could do, our son grabbed the two suggestions of feet and legs that were sticking out by then, and pulled with all his might, as the cow just stood there acting like it was all in a day's work. After a concerted effort at pulling that calf into the light of day, she arrived. A nice, big, healthy heifer calf. And what a welcome into the world—a plop onto the hay-covered ground from about chest height. And the cow remained standing up the whole time to have her baby, barely flinching as it was all taking place behind her.

Big show off.

It's always amazing to see the instincts of baby animals kick in—holding their heads up right away, standing within 20-30 minutes, knowing where to look to get something to eat. It was all pretty mesmerizing until the cow discovered all that "other stuff" on the ground that is part of the birthing process, and started snacking, as farm animals do.

Somehow, my high school Home Economics class didn't prepare me for that.

This column by Karen Schwaller first appeared in *Farm News*.

LOADING HOGS: DEAD OR ALIVE

I would hear the words now and then, and they would never cease to strike a certain fear in me and send me into a cold sweat. At first I thought it was the beginning of menopause, but then it dawned on me that each time I would hear my husband utter the words, "I sold hogs for tomorrow," all the symptoms would reappear.

The arduous job of loading hogs has to rate right up there with cleaning toilets; it's not the most glamorous job there is, but it's a necessary job that must be done. The only difference is that it takes a lot fewer naughty words to accomplish the toilet cleaning task than it does to get the trailer door shut behind 24 head of market hogs.

Miraculous things happen on market day on the farm. The husband you chose becomes transformed into someone or something you've never seen before. They say the weather in Iowa changes quickly; the same holds true for marital relationships if husband and wives load hogs together very often. It goes without saying that marital status could be directly related to the ease in which the hogs load.

Once everything is in place, the marking and sorting begins. Children often learn the hard way that they should have had the gate either open or shut, depending on what we're trying to do. The experts say, "You have to learn to think like a hog." I don't think I've mastered that one yet, and I'm not sure if it's a bad thing.

One-liners run rampant. The best one is, "Watch that hog!" as your farmer comes to mark one out of a group, and all ten of them try to rush the gate out of which you're sorting. That's high anxiety, because they all look the same to me.

Usually at least one of our children would end up riding a pig backwards before the sorting process was through. It looked kind of funny, but made me shudder at the same time to think about what could happen. To them it was great fun when it happened. To me it meant I probably wouldn't know what I'll look like when I'm seventy because hog loading and all that goes with it has taken years off my lifespan.

Before long, it's time to begin loading them. Everyone is strategically placed behind the hogs and alongside the chute—sorting panels, whips and the stock prod in hand, and our best hog-calling voices ready to go. What a sight we must be.

Once it begins, there is no going back. The pigs start up the loading chute. After one pig turns around and forgets how to walk forward, therein lies the seed that sprouts the transformation process of what was once the husband you knew.

First it begins with some inaudible, colorful language as my husband separates himself from the head-end of the hog with the thickness of a sorting panel. It's a test of wills as he tries to get the pig to advance down the chute. As their heads butt, the prod comes out and the language gets a little louder. Before long, the shouting begins. The pig(s) in the chute are barking and wound up.

And so is everyone else.

The neighbors half a mile away must rush their small children indoors and close the windows on hog loading day at our house, because I'm certain they can hear every word.

The real fun begins when the pigs jump over the side of the chute. That usually only happens after my husband has lost the battle—trying to keep it in the chute by grabbing the pig's ears and pulling them in the direction he needs the pig to go. For a moment or two my husband and the pig are the same height as he tips the pig over in the right direction. As the kids grew, they tried more and more to keep them from jumping over the chute as their level of bravery increased. But sorting panels held in place by growing hands are little match for an angry, 250-pound pig. Most of the time, they (smartly) just got out of the way.

Between the wound-up pigs and now, a wound-up father, the kids are usually in tears before it's over. Learning on the job is tough, especially when you're a kid . . . or the wife.

After the trailer door is closed behind the last one and the calm after the storm has set in, it's obvious that loading hogs isn't a job for weenies or the weak of heart. Apologies are made, tears are dried and wedding vows are still holding, if only by the thread of a twine string.

For our kids when they were growing up, the ride to the sale barn was enough to make them forget about what it took to get there in the first place. It truly is hog heaven for them.

One time we had a pig that died in the hog house. After it was gutted out, we maneuvered the pickup to the spot where it laid, and loaded it up. We then clumsily swung the carcass around to get it where it needed to be.

"This kind loads better than the lives ones," my husband joked.

It was true. And we stayed friends the whole time loading it.

This column by Karen Schwaller first
appeared in *Farm News.*

AN UNDERRATED JOB—MOTHER'S DAY THOUGHTS

I truly believe that while God calls specific men and women to serve in His church, God also calls specific women to become farm wives and farm mothers.

What other excuse is there for doing it this long? I'd certainly hate for others to think I actually chose this kind of life—the endless days, the manure-covered clothes in the washer, hogs with an attitude (directly relating to hog producers with an attitude); supper served at dark-thirty, and hoping you don't smell like the barn when you go somewhere because of an unexpected chase scene minutes before you leave.

Farm wives and mothers are unique indeed, wearing many hats in a day. They can nurse sick kids and sick livestock all at once, feed kids and animals as needed, run a taxi service for kids and drive a tractor, clean the house and clean out the barn. She can guide her children along the path of life and guide the hogs up the loading chute. She is a sounding board to soothe a farmer's ire when things go wrong, and can come out fighting like a mother bear when she feels like she needs to. She plays the role of business partner, finance manager and will even play cowboys with her own little ones when they run one cowboy short for their herd.

Along with the status of farm mother comes the direct correlation of being married to a farmer, which could in some instances, automatically put some farm wives up for instant sainthood. After all, there are things she must endure that other wives wouldn't necessarily have to think about, largely because she is married to a very practical and very busy man.

I chuckle when I think of a conversation I heard once between a farmer and his wife as her birthday approached.

"What do you want for your birthday?" he inquired.

"Well . . . if I have to plug it in, I don't want it. And if you can buy it from a hardware store and deduct it from our taxes, I don't want that either," she said, hinting at something a little less useful, as women sometimes like.

For my own birthday a few years ago, my husband—who actually remembered my birthday during the rush of the fall harvest season—got me my own pair of insulated coveralls. While I was quite happy to have them, I told him how brave he must have been entering no-man's land and picking out a size for me.

Lucky for him, he chose coveralls that were too small for me.

A little flattery now and then never hurts, does it?? A brief exchange at the store, and I was warm and comfortable working outside that winter, and everyone was happy.

It's my belief that the job of farm mother has been underrated as well. Only a farm mom could usher a heavily-manure-speckled little boy into the house, clean him up and have the nerve to kiss him good night an hour later. She's talented enough to put a bean head on a toy combine for an impatient five-year-old while she does aerobics in the living room, and hears from time to time as she cuts her young son's hair that the hair clipper ". . . looks like a corn head."

You can take the boy out of the country, but it's true—you can't take the country out of some boys.

Only a farm mom can assert such a logical thought process to a rambunctious child, saying firmly, "If you're going to fall and crack your head open, please wait until I get done scraping out this farrowing house so I'll have the time to take you to the hospital."

I believe it was Ed Dussalt who said, "If evolution really works, how come mothers have only two hands?"

But it was an anonymously written ditty which caught my eye one day while thumbing through a magazine. It read, "Automation is a technological process that does all the work while you just sit there. When you were younger, this was called 'Mother.'"

So to moms on and off the farm this Mother's Day, I wish you a day filled with happy times, great memories, the satisfaction that comes with doing your job well and gifts that don't plug in or can't be deducted from your farm taxes.

This column by Karen Schwaller first
appeared in *Farm News*.

THE FARM HOUSE

Is it the difference between houses in town and houses on the farm, or is it the difference between the people who inhabit them?

The longer I live on the farm, the more I learn about the practicality of not only farm families, but of the houses which shelter them from the perils of Mother Nature.

The difference was once made clear a few years ago upon the arrival of one of our daughter's friends, who lived in town. This third-grade girl made her way inside the door, wrinkled her nose and ran like a gazelle out of the nose-burning range.

She said, "Your house smells bad."

It reminded me of one summer when I was working at the local newspaper office, and after arriving at work, I had put on some perfume. Shortly afterwards, a woman from next door came in, noticed the aroma and, after hesitating, inquired, "Fly spray?"

I never wore that perfume again.

While the little girl visiting our house found it incredulous to think that we who live here hardly even notice the obnoxious odors emanating from the rinsed-off, yet once-swine-poop-laden boots in the basement, she was anxious to help our kids do their chores—something she never had the opportunity to do at home.

She needed a chore coat, so I handed her an everyday one we had hanging in our basement by all the other everyday boots and overalls.

She got one arm halfway into the sleeve, then said, "I think I'll wear my own coat. This one stinks." (I didn't' tell her that she

18

would probably smell the same way by the time she was finished.)

Is it really that bad? Or are farm people born with desensitized noses?

Farm kids usually just get dressed in their chore clothes and get the lead out—possibly because most of the time they smell as bad as the coat. If not initially, then eventually.

Elsewhere in our house, the bathroom has been a makeshift hospital for sick and cold baby lambs and pigs, and our utility room in the basement has also served as an operating room for pigs that need to be stitched up and kept away from the constant nudging of other pigs.

We've had sick, newborn lambs in the bathtub to get them warmed up, and when we have run out of room in the farrowing house in the fall and winter, we've been known to replace the car in the garage with a pig mover hooked onto the tractor so a sow could have pigs in a warm place.

Farm families truly know that their own needs come second to the needs of those they have committed themselves to caring for—especially if those beings have four legs.

Our basement is stocked with all kinds of things found in other farm business ventures, including boxes full of right-handed work gloves, boots (with one of most pairs having a tiny but very real hole in it, first discovered while stepping into liquid manure); a stock prod that needs a bath, a refrigerator that resembles a mini veterinarian's office; and at times a feeder box—which a farmer will occasionally build in the basement during the winter to replace the one on the feeder outside, which he didn't have time to fix during the summer or fall.

But most of all, farm houses are full of young children's treasures—found outside in their adventures of work or play. There are "real cool rocks;" twine strings—which their father has carefully instructed them to place in the back pocket of their coveralls so they don't get caught in the skid loader or the lawn mower blades. There are handfuls of straw, fireflies in jars, captured tadpoles and frogs, cattails, corn that they need to haul in by the pocketsful and use with their farm toy wagons and elevators; and at least a million different kinds of seed corn caps—all of which they couldn't possibly live without.

One of the most unusual things I'd ever found while raking the mud out of the basement was a lamb's tail, which had fallen off of one of their baby lambs. After my initial shock, I decided I was okay with it, as long as I didn't find the lamb secretly living somewhere in the basement.

I probably wouldn't notice the smell, anyway.

This column by Karen Schwaller first
appeared in *Farm News*.

DRIVING MACHINERY AND
OTHER MOM WORRIES

The more I invest in this thing called marriage and family, the more I understand why some people skip the whole process and go right into training for neurosurgery.

It's a lot easier.

When it comes right down to it, there are some fundamental differences in the way men and women think. Men wonder how women can change a baby's soiled diaper without a gas mask and garden hose in close proximity, and women wonder how men can think that way about changing a diaper, then turn around and be up to their shoulders pulling a baby pig out of its troubled mother, or fixing a prolapse without visually revisiting what they had to eat at their last meal.

At our house, I had been wondering why the dad was in such a hurry for the kids to grow up, while the dad was finally realizing the true value of all those piles of spit-up laundry and cloth diapers I washed, and of all the nights he slept through the 2 a.m. feedings. After all, the kids were growing up and they were becoming much more useful than they had been in the crib.

It came out of the blue, as most unexpected things do. I'd just returned from a long day on the job and had dialed up my husband that evening to see what was happening. He was out harvesting.

"You won't' believe it, but the boys are running the grain carts."

Our boys were 10 years old then, and after already spending a lot of harvest seasons out riding in the tractors and seeing how it's all done, they had been hounding their dad to see when they could start helping with the harvest. Knowing that I didn't think much of the idea, my husband had put it off—or he had until that day.

"They're doing what?" I asked, hoping I'd somehow gotten some post-ceremony rice in my ear that day as I took wedding pictures.

"They're running the grain carts—dumping on the go and everything. They're having a blast, and they're doing a really nice job," my husband answered in a state of fatherly pride and excitement. "They've been running them all day."

Eventually, farm mothers have to face this day, knowing all that could happen. It's just that the day arrives much sooner than expected . . . and for fathers, well . . . the day is finally here.

When I was able to get out to the field with them the following weekend, one of our sons was anxious to give me a ride, showing me that he was capable of doing a man's work. "Did you come so I could give you a ride? Please??" he asked.

With a grin and a bounce in his step (unlike that which we would see as he would meet the school bus), we headed toward the very large red tractor which was hooked up to a very large red grain cart. He hopped into the tractor like he'd done it a gazillion times, and slid way over.

"Jeepers—how big do you think my butt is?" I teased.

"Well I was just sliding over so you could get in," he said.

"You have a lot to learn about women, young man," I said as I winked and closed the door behind me, sitting down next to him.

He grinned at me, and we started on our trek toward the combine. Next, he got on the radio. "Where do you want the grain cart?" he asked the man who farmed the field.

"Just put 'er on the west end," he instructed. Which our son did.

(I was 30 years old before I could tell you which end of the field would be the west end.)

He waited for the combine, then started down the rows alongside it, catching the corn in the cart as they went down the rows together. When the signal was given that the cart was full, he pulled away from the combine and headed for the semi, where my husband was waiting to unload the cart for him.

"Aren't they doing a nice job?" he asked.

I had to admit that they were. Later that night when they all got home, my husband came in tired, took his cap off to scratch his head, put his lunch pail in the kitchen and yawned as he headed for the shower.

There were two shorter versions of him that did exactly the same thing. It was so funny.

It worked out fine, but the mother in me couldn't help but think that if our husbands had our job in the delivery room and the nine months before it, they wouldn't be in such a hurry for them to grow up either. That's why, for the first time in a long time, I played with their farm set-up in our front porch. It was like the beginning of the end of an era. But before I was done, in an attempt to tease them I mixed up their pigs and cattle, tipped over some of the fences and opened gates so it looked like the animals could get out.

When they discovered it a couple of days later, I told them that if they were going to be gone farming, they had to learn to make sure everything at home was taken care of first, so it didn't make a bunch of extra work for people. They just grinned at me.

Someday I'm going to miss those grins.

This column by Karen Schwaller first appeared
in the *Sioux City Journal.*

THE BAD WEEK

It doesn't take us long in this life to figure out that there are days and weeks that contribute highly to both our income and inner peace; they may even feign productiveness. And that there are other days and weeks that are simply thrust upon us—much like Iowa winters, taxes and mending day on the farm—and all we can do is meet those challenges head on and hope we can endure the storm.

Our boys had such a week during harvest. And in usual Schwaller style, they didn't have an assortment of piddly things happen—that just wouldn't be true to the name.

As the week began, one of our boys was moving grain trucks around in the field, and backed one into their farm pickup. Didn't do great damage, but enough to show some prestigious war wounds. Now they have been initiated into that elite club of truck drivers.

They also had a couple of small fires to extinguish on their (new to them) combine, and even got their combine stuck in the mud a couple of times during that week. By that Tuesday night, it had already been a week not to be believed.

The call came from the sheriff's office at 1:30 a.m. that Wednesday morning, asking if some cows that were out belonged to us. The location was described, and I said they most likely were ours. (They belonged to our sons.) One had been hit by a truck. So we were all out of the house in five minutes and headed over to the pasture, where the sheriff's deputies were waiting for us with lights flashing in the quiet darkness of the night, keeping the cows off of the road.

We saw the cow that had been hit sitting up in the ditch, and worked most immediately on keeping the others off of the road and getting them into temporary shelter for the night. Thank God for Iowa farm people who will answer their door at 2 a.m. without a gun or baseball bat—as our sons asked them for a place for their cows to stay for the night.

It seemed almost "Mary-and-Joseph"-like.

Once their shelter was secured, we went back over to the injured cow, and discovered that it was one of our boys' most prized cows—a heifer they named Thelma. Thelma was no ordinary heifer; she had been born one of twin heifers a year and a half ago to a cow that they received as payment for some summer work. Their young mother had died unexpectedly and left her two little calves behind—which the boys bottle fed from that time on. Twin boys feeding twin heifer bottle calves—they already had that special connection. Aside from the reason they had to feed them, they enjoyed that time spent together, and quickly became friends.

One son choked back tears as he could see that she was seriously hurt, and that she would most likely not recover. Still, he rubbed her head and, I'm guessing, silently began his farewells to her at that moment, in the quietness of a dark and deserted country road; also mourning what could have been.

She could sit up somewhat, but it was obvious that she was not going to be able to stand. So the boys and their dad literally lifted Thelma up and placed her into the trailer so we could bring her home. They got her some water, tried to make her comfortable, and stayed with her.

Around 5 a.m., one of our sons came to tell us that Thelma had died.

"What do you think we should do with her?" he asked, though he knew full well the answer that would come.

After some discussion between him and his dad, it was decided that if they could at least get the meat from her, they wouldn't be left with nothing to show for all of the work they had put into her until then. And so it was decided. The boys went to get the tractor and loader to hang her up and get her ready.

Farm kids know from a young age what livestock is grown for, and that all farm animals eventually end up on someone's plate. But when that animal is also a friend, it's a mournful time no matter who you are . . . or how old you are.

I heard the tractor, and it broke my heart to know why they needed it. Yet I couldn't even begin to imagine the pain the boys were enduring as they got ready to prepare one of their favorite cows—who had become more like a dog to them by way of companionship—for slaughter.

The deed was done, but not without tears and visible sorrow. All of this, and it was barely daybreak. When the time was right, a sample of meat was harvested from her so we could try it out to see if the meat would be edible, given the circumstances under which she had died.

My husband grilled the meat that evening, and we all sat down together at the table. But this time was different than any other meal we'd shared together. This time we had known our main entrée.

We all placed some meat on our plates, and sat there for a moment before one of the boys said, "I don't know if I can eat my bottle calf."

Following some silence and eyes that looked at our food somehow differently, their dad took a bite; slowly and gingerly, the rest of us picked up our silverware and did as well. It was a very quiet supper, filled with memories of a lost friend.

Four-legged friends are hard to lose, too. We're just glad that week is over.

This column by Karen Schwaller first
appeared in *Farm News*.

SALE DAY AT THE FAIR

Livestock sale day at the fair.

The words alone are enough to make you want to go running into the cellar—because you know the storm is coming. People with kids in 4-H and FFA get quiet when they hear the words, especially if they have experienced it before. Once you have experienced that with your kids, you are never the same.

Livestock sale day has kind of a love-hate thing going. The kids raise their animals and sell them to make some money, but unlike with livestock at home, they have to spend a little extra time with those animals—washing them, breaking them to lead, becoming friends with them. And while they are excited to get a little cash from selling their animals at the fair, it also means a farewell comes between the show arena and the truck that awaits them outside the barns.

4-H and FFA kids get up early that morning—usually a little earlier than normal—probably because they didn't sleep well that night before, knowing what they have to do the next morning. They arrive at the fairgrounds to wash and prepare their animals one last time, maybe with a little more care than they washed and prepared them before. Soon they hear the sound of trucks coming onto the fairgrounds, and even the youngest 4-H'ers know what they are for. The crowd and the bidders arrive, and all too soon they hear the sound of the auctioneer's voice, and someone calling out their name, saying that they are on deck to take their animal into the sale ring.

I have always been kind of glad that I have had a camera to hide behind as our kids entered the sale ring. It was plain to see how hard it was for them to sell their animals, as it was for many 4-H and FFA kids each year. Some go through the ring like it's all in a day's work; but for others who have truly spent quality time with their animals and become friends, it's a swan song of sorts. One that is made through misty eyes, and sometimes outright tears before a crowd of bidders and spectators. And many of those people watching are also choking back tears. They are probably parents of 4-H and FFA kids too, who know how hard this day is for the kids—and for the families.

My husband—an avid supporter of the FFA program—was one of the FFA kids who helped out on sale day at the fair one year when he was in high school. Someone asked him to help in the beef barn that day, and so he did. But he said it didn't take long to figure out that it was going to be a very difficult morning—with the somber mood in the beef barn, and the tears it took for kids (and even sometimes dads) to bring their calves back through the barn, remove their halters one last time, and say their farewells as the truck awaited them.

My husband learned a lot that day as a high school FFA member who—although he was raising his own livestock at the time, had never shown an animal at the fair.

For young 4-H'ers, they often get their first taste of it with sheep or goats that they bring to the fair. They're both great young-kid projects, and it's hard not to become attached to something you have raised from the time it was born. For our own young kids at the time, those first sheep were hard to let go.

For older kids especially, it seems to be the calf sale that matters most. Some hide behind their calves while the auctioneer does his job, while others lead their calves around bravely, or even with open tears.

It's a hard thing to watch, but it's also heartwarming to know that these kids have done the work that 4-H and FFA asks of them—to care for their animals. If they didn't, it wouldn't be so hard to say farewell to them on the last day.

This year I heard one of the sheep committee guys say after the sheep in the barn had all been loaded up, "Nothing's left but the tears." Truer words were never spoken.

Did I mention anything about hogs here? Well, this all holds true except for hogs.

Over in the swine barn, the kids mechanically help shoo them up the chute and into the truck—hopefully not using the same language their dads use while doing that same job at home. No kids seem to miss their hogs—they just want the cash.

Two different neighborhood philosophers shared some tidbits of porcine knowledge with me; one told me that if a hog had a head on both ends, it would go sideways.

And the other once told me that getting people to move in a line is worse than working with hogs. "You can't lead 'em, and you can't drive 'em," he explained.

If only we could think of that on livestock sale day at the fair.

This column by Karen Schwaller first
appeared in *Farm News*.

FARM PHRASE-OLOGY, BY THE NUMBERS

I t's part of living on the farm . . . those often-repeated phrases that farmers have a way of coining. Any farm wife can probably tell you that over time, she could compile a list of the ones she cringes at the most.

At the Schwaller farm, there are several on that list—some dreaded more than others—but this should provide most would-be farm wives with the most common phrases they need to be aware of. They are written from ten-word phrases down to one-word phrases.

Here we go—

*TEN WORDS: "Don't throw that away—I might need it for something." This could perhaps be a farm wife's worst nightmare, for after the farmer runs out of room in the machine shed and any other shed in which he's been saving things, he invariably begins smuggling things into the house. The solution? With all the money he's saved on junk that's beginning to grow over there in the corner of the machine shed, he could afford to build you a new and bigger house . . . you know, so he has enough room to store his stuff, of course.

*NINE WORDS: "Can you run to town to get a part?" Here's a biggie. There have probably been three farm wives since the invention of them who have come home with the right part every time they have gone after one. Even though my husband knows he's time and money ahead just to get these things himself, every now and then he still asks me to do the honor. It helps to buy yourself a new outfit before you leave town so it won't be an entirely wasted trip.

*EIGHT WORDS (spoken at 11:30 a.m.): "There'll be three extra people here for dinner." This isn't so bad when you had a big roast in the oven anyway, but when you were planning on leftovers for the family, it's grounds for some kind of, well, 'discussion' after the kids have gone to bed, since you didn't have time for that to happen when he first told you—because you had to dream up some kind of miracle meal.

*SEVEN WORDS: "I might need your help after a while." These can be extremely suspicious words, and any farm wife who hears them should be immediately aware that she could be getting herself involved in jobs that could eventually lead to the demise of the marriage if the project doesn't go well. Find out first how much he values the relationship and don't do anything without first signing a "pre-swine-moving agreement. Everyone knows how THAT job goes.

*SIX WORDS: "They charged how much for this?" He says angrily and with knitted eyebrows pointed right at you. The solution? Refer back to phrase number nine and tell him to do his own shopping from now on.

*FIVE WORDS: "I sold hogs for tomorrow." This is a tricky one indeed. While the money is usually needed and spent before it arrives, the process of loading hogs can be pricey for the farmer and his wife. Make sure all life insurance premiums have been paid up before entering into this kind of adrenaline-laden, shout-driven activity—and remember that loading hogs without a stock prod is like trying to sew while wearing oven mitts.

*FOUR WORDS: "I lost my pliers." These are four of the most frustrating words a farmer can utter. Pliers to a farmer are equivalent to silverware at meal times—they can't work without them. Unless you love sewing through leather, umpteen layers of denim or insulated coveralls, keep a steady supply of pliers in your stash of "things that make it all better."

*THREE WORDS: "Watch that hog!" This is usually spoken so fast and so ferociously that it sounds like he's speaking in the tongue of some ancient civilization. Usually, the phrase is useless because it's spoken most often as the one hog he wants to keep back is making its way through the sorting gate you're watching—or supposed to be watching.

*TWO WORDS: "Loose hogs." Whether it means the pigs got out, or whether they are producing three times the manure they usually do—in any sense of the word, it means more work for everyone. Exercise regularly to keep a strong heart for the arduous job of chasing hogs, and—well, keep a strong shovel and lots of laundry soap on hand for the other part.

*ONE WORD: "Fieldwork." To a farm wife, this means turning her kitchen into a short-order restaurant on wheels and adds a whole new meaning to 'rustling up some grub.' Keep plenty of food in the kitchen, gas in the chuck wagon, and have two hands ready to help when things aren't going as planned— which you can usually plan on.

Happy farming. And farm wives, buck up. You've got the winter off.

This column by Karen Schwaller first
appeared in *Farm News.*

OFF TO COLLEGE FOR THE FIRST TIME

I've decided that it's just a weekend that parents need to get through . . . to endure.

This past fall, we entered the ranks of those sending their first born off to college. And because our daughter is as grown-up as can be, it was as easy as it was difficult.

If you've sent one off to college, you know what I mean. You spend their senior year in your own world of excitement and maybe even a little grief—thinking about what is to come for them and for you—and realizing that you only have a couple more years left to be able to say that your gut is really still baby fat leftover from pregnancy.

(Dads, too bad that one only works for moms . . .)

I've come a long way since my own graduation almost thirty years ago. Coming from a family of seven children, our parents each gave us at graduation time a suitcase and a clock radio. They were the most practical of gifts for the graduate, and were highly used. But looking back from the parental side now, one couldn't help but think that, as each child graduated and left home, those gifts said, "You're done sponging off of us now. So go find your own place, get a job and don't be late for work."

I even got a smaller suitcase for my eighth grade graduation. I should have seen it coming even then.

It had to be our parents' little slice of heaven—whittling down the list of kids left at home each year, and dreaming about being empty nesters. We probably didn't see the party dancing that went on as they saw our tail lights in the driveway.

I read once that, "God gives us teenagers so that it won't be so hard for us when they leave home." While that may be true for some, it didn't ring very true at our house.

We were blessed with a beautiful baby girl, who grew into a very beautiful young woman, right before our eyes, and almost overnight. She is the kind of daughter that we could never have hoped to have, because she ended up being more than we ever wished for.

When it came time for her to leave home and pursue a future that included studying agriculture, it was something she looked forward to with great anticipation and readiness—and her father looked to it with great pride, since it was always his dream to raise his family on a farm.

And while we were happy for her, my husband and I were a little weirded-out that we had officially entered this part of our lives. We knew it would come, and we know that we don't raise kids to keep them. But it still got here much sooner than we expected.

Mothers push babies into the world, but fathers push children into the world. In this case, giving our daughter the responsibilities of life on the farm, and in turn, a vocation.

Summer came and went, and we anticipated her needs for college. We made lists, the likes of those never seen by Mr. S. Claus at the North Pole. We bought and packed her things, and finally it was time to load them into vehicles and make the 2 ½-hour drive to college . . . to a world that, for the first time, we really weren't going to know.

We got her moved into her dorm room, and finally it was time to go. How strange it felt being the ones to leave her while she was the one who stayed behind.

We got through the farewells, but it didn't come without some stomach aches and sadness at the thought of leaving her there, even though we knew she was very ready for this step. We hugged her—perhaps more profoundly than before—and wished her well, though misty eyes that we tried hard not to show. No one wanted to make it harder on the other.

Later that fall, I remembered that day as I watched a scene unfold at a preschool door. A little girl sporting a backpack was crying and hugging her mother's neck ferociously as she sobbed, "Mommy I don't wanna go!" The mother hugged her, stroked her hair gently and said, "I'll come back for you, honey. I always come back for you, don't I?"

It made me remember that day we left our daughter at college those weeks earlier. It also made me think of the irony in that scene as the mother comforted her daughter, saying she would be back. When we left our daughter, there were some crocodile tears in the room as our daughter hugged our necks and assured us that she would be back.

We had discovered how much we needed each other.

That circle of life was beginning to close in, and somehow her words of assurance didn't help us any more than those words from her mother helped that little preschool girl that day.

But walking away, we closed that chapter in our lives and began the next one—knowing that we did all we could to give her roots. It was time for her wings to fly now.

We could never have understood in the delivery room how difficult that would be for us . . . and how wonderful, too.

This column by Karen Schwaller first
appeared in *Farm News*.

FARM WIFE GETS EDUCATION IN FIELD WORK

As a kid growing up with four brothers who did all the farming with my dad, "field work" for me consisted of walking beans and picking up rocks . . . and I didn't always get in on the rock-picking escapades.

Field work, now that I was a little older and married, meant occasionally climbing onto the tractor for a few hours of terror-induced fidgeting mixed with some welcome peace and quiet.

How my father must have loved an afternoon of disking or field cultivating all those years ago, with nothing but the sound of a finely-tuned tractor, an implement, and the velvety tones emerging from the country-western station on the fender-mounted tractor radio—free from the relentless bickering of seven growing children. Heaven was only as far away as his tractor.

Well, after having married a farmer myself, I figured the day would come when I'd have to learn the tricks of the field work trade. That time did soon arrive.

"Do you want to do some disking this afternoon, dear? I'll show you everything you need to know," he crooned.

"Mmm, okay," I replied in a somewhat carefree manner, hoping he wouldn't notice the table moving as a result of my trembling knees beneath it.

All intentions were good, but by the time I got to the field after my own obligations were completed, my husband had about 10 minutes to teach me the things he'd considered second nature on the old 190 Allis Chalmers. My eyes were spinning as he as he quickly recited his "Ten Commandments For Disking."

"If the oil light comes on, don't look around for the problem first—shut off the tractor right away. If the hydraulics leak, check the hoses over and drive slowly to the bin, then shut it off. If the hydraulics are running out the bottom of the tractor, shut if off right away. If you lose power steering it means you're losing oil. And be sure keep the RPMs at this range while you're disking," he said, pointing to the dial behind the steering wheel. "Oh, and don't forget to look behind you once in a while to make sure the disk is still hooked onto the tractor."

It would be years later before I would imagine all of these potential problems happening to my own aging body, and the time it would take to check all of that.

Truly, I was less confused at the height of the Whitewater scandal.

After a couple of frighteningly educational rounds, my husband was off to his own obligations—leaving me alone with a moody tractor and the old, small disk—surrounded by fields being smoothed with disks that covered vast amounts of acres in a single round, and hooked onto new green and red tractors.

I knew if I made a glaring error I'd be the talk of the neighborhood. The good thing was that they would think it was my husband doing it and not me—it was a win-win situation all around for me. Even so, it was still a scary thought being the new kid on the block—or the new kid on the block's somewhat paranoid wife.

Having only one problem at the beginning (which necessitated my husband turning around after half a mile and returning to the field), I began disking on my own.

My eyes were kept busy between the field, disk, hydraulic lines, the RPM monitor, the oil light, and watching the neighbors in the surrounding fields whom I imagined were watching me since I was new to the field neighborhood.

I didn't dare listen to the radio for fear of being distracted; I didn't want to end up on the news, ya know?

But luck treated me much better than it did my husband just hours before when he was disking because I didn't have a single problem. In fact, I had the audacity to almost enjoy what I was doing, even if I didn't always know what I was doing. Before long I just knew the whine of the tractor when I reached the correct

RPM, and a glance at the monitor showed me I was right each time.

I dared to get cocky enough to sing aloud in the cab as I drove along; heck, I even swooped around a couple of times after I was already done, just for the fun of it.

Surely, I thought, I had crossed that line between farm wife and farmer. I imagined myself wearing a seed corn cap, greasy jeans and fuel-soaked gloves for the rest of my life . . . right before I swerved the tractor away from the fenceline.

Seriously, though, I'd gone full circle in a single afternoon, from heart palpitations and slight nausea to making myself quit when I was done.

Unbelievable.

I parked the tractor, went home and washed off the afternoon's coating of dirt, grease, grime and diesel fuel, and called my husband.

"How'd it go?" he asked with more curiosity than optimism.

"I got done," I beamed.

"No kidding?!" he replied incredulously, with a nervous laugh. "I'd have never guessed you'd get it done."

"I am woman," I mused, feeling a little bit like Helen Reddy. "Now what should I do with the tractor?" (The weather was cold.)

"Plug it in," he said. "The plug-in is right behind the block."

"Where's the block?" I asked, feeling like my Helen Reddy status was going to be short-lived.

"It's between the hood and the frame," he tried to explain.

(Sigh . . .) This farming thing is gonna take some learning . . . and a lot of aspirin, I think.

This column by Karen Schwaller first appeared
in the *Sioux City Journal.*

FARMING THE LIVING ROOM CARPET

When the month of July hits, field work has been running rampant for a couple of months. And if you have young farm children who idolize their farming father, you know how difficult it can be just to walk through your house come spring.

It's not the usual post-winter, early-spring clutter you can usually find lying around our house that time of year—the abandoned stocking hats and insulated coveralls strewn about, the Christmas cards you meant to get sent before then, or even Aunt Edna—who may or may not be officially classified as "clutter that's lying around the house."

It used to be the farm implements that would get dragged into our living room by four growing, pre-school hands that were anxious to do the real thing someday; powered by four bare knees plodding on the carpet through the holes in their jeans. (Disclaimer: Holes in the knees of jeans in this story is in no way an indication of the overall job of mending I do on the farm.)

As soon as our young sons would hear their dad utter something about getting the planter out of the machine shed, they left us in a cloud of dust on their way to the front porch—where they would get their own line of machinery out of their own machine shed.

(Disclaimer: The aforementioned "cloud of dust" may or may not occur indoors. The names have been changed to protect the domestically challenged.)

I've often wondered how many years a living room carpet can be farmed. From the time our young boys were big enough to hold onto a tractor and know what it was for, they've made countless rounds in the living room and dining room—growing everything from soybeans to corn, hay, rye and Froot Loops. And our carpet shows it.

The hitches on the implements (or "hookers," as they would call them) would always get caught in the carpet strands, causing them to stretch out longer than the other fibers. I felt like a Christopher Columbus-era beautician—giving a flat-headed hair trim in a round-headed world.

At times it could even be handy having them farm our living room carpet. If sometime we were having company and I didn't have time to vacuum, I could tell our boys to disk over the carpet a few times to make those marks that the disks make.

"How do you have time to get your housework done?" the guests would ask as they look at what appears to be a freshly-vacuumed carpet, while the cobwebs dangle just inches above their heads.

"Oh, the boys do it," I'd lie, serving a two-fold purpose. I'd look like a June Cleaver housekeeper while giving the impression that the boys have learned to take on household responsibilities.

Back and forth they go—disking, planting, and spraying with a homemade sprayer made of yogurt cartons, rubber bands and a wire. (They watch their father closely as he creates agricultural masterpieces out of nothing.) They bale, combine and clean out the barn with a skid loader and spread manure. Heaven, for them, is as far away as their farm toys—second only to the real thing.

But someday the reality of buying new carpet is going to hit, because what we have now will someday be placed in permanent CRP—the Carpet Replacement Pile.

I always imagined that the trip to the carpet store could be interesting.

"May I help you?" asks the store clerk.

"Yes, I need some new carpet for my living room and dining room," I'd reply. "The carpet I have now has gone through one too many plantings and harvests."

"Yes, I know all about that," the store clerk would say. "My husband farms, too. There's so much corn ground into the carpet."

"My biggest trouble is all of the hookers that get stuck in the carpet strands," I would inform her.

This would be followed by a look of shock and shame from the store clerk.

"And not only that, but I need a carpet that can stand up to tillage and planting every year. It's looking pretty thin in places, especially where they pile the manure out of their barn."

"You allow that on your carpet??" she would ask incredulously.

"Well, they have to go somewhere with it," I'd reply. "I just tell them to put it over in the corner until they get time to spread it somewhere."

"You don't mind all of this going on in your home?" she would ask in a bewildered tone, politely stepping away from me, thinking I have manure somewhere on me.

"Heck, you're only young once," I'd tell her. "You can always get new carpeting."

The store clerk faints.

One time when the kids were very little I came into the house looking for something, and I found a pair of shoes filled with corn inside the door of the porch. I followed a trail of corn through the living room up the stairs, through the hallway and into the boys' bedroom. I could have popped a cork upon seeing all of that on the floor that I'd just cleaned. Instead, the boys "harvested" that corn by hand that night.

Now when they talk to their grandfathers they can say they've done that, too . . . just as long as they don't ask them if their hookers ever got caught in the carpet.

No siree. Maybe they'd better just silently wonder that one; especially in the presence of Grandma.

This column by Karen Schwaller first appeared in *Farm News*.

BREAKING THE CALF

Our kids are all nine-year veterans of the 4-H program in our county. Over the years we've seen them work on and show a lot of exhibits, and probably none have been as frustrating—nor as popular—with them as their livestock exhibits.

For those of you who have never experienced the process of getting those animals to the fair, let it be known right now that there are some things mothers just tolerate, and other things that they plainly should not see.

Fair time approaching usually meant that I could reach underneath the sink to seize the dish soap, but it didn't mean that it was always there. Fair time meant phantom dish soap—I knew it should be there, but I could never see it. Typically, it would be out by the hydrant where they were washing sheep and calves, and all that was left under our kitchen sink was dishwashing dreams and spiders which had probably lived there since the Nixon administration.

And then, there was breaking those sheep and calves to lead. Thus, the one thing that mothers should not watch.

Around the Schwallers', breaking sheep and calves to lead was something that was typically not done until shortly before the fair. We wouldn't want to begin the process too early—it just wouldn't be true Schwaller style to begin something in a timely manner.

One evening in an outright display of mental instability, I sashayed out to watch one of our sons break his calf to lead. The weather was gorgeous and I was looking forward to seeing how the whole process worked from the beginning—so I climbed up on the fence to watch. The other calves were leading well by then, but this one had some extra snort and a gangster-like attitude. It acted like it should be coming out of a chute—rider on top with a hand in the air.

Some fancy roping resulted in getting a halter of sorts on; that was the last time I remembered being content with watching what went on in that self-made rodeo.

Our son clutched the rope as some role reversal started things out, with the calf leading him around for a while. There was much chasing around, and all of a sudden the calf took off, our son hanging onto the rope, and it looked like a new Olympic ski sport had been born—Manure Mogels. Our son displayed quite show of athletic prowess—demonstrating strength, balance and tenacity as he hung with the cow, sliding on his heels in the greasy . . . well, okay . . . and determined to win this one. I was praying he would let go before something happened, but just that quick, the cow stopped to rest, and our son slid to a stop.

Actually, my heart needed that rest more than that cow did.

Pulling on the rope to show the cow his disgust with that rather bossy display, our son was able to slowly approach the cow again. It spun around—this time, slamming our son up against a nearby building and keeping him there for a short time.

As he calmly and mechanically separated himself from the calf and the building, I was beginning to think about that John Wayne movie, *The Cowboys,* and how our kids must have watched that at least a gazillion times before they got old enough to go to kindergarten. Somehow this looked so much easier in the movies.

Our son landed against the side of that same building a second time, and luckily, his cell phone and a ripped pair of blue jeans were the only near casualties of that incident. The phone still worked, but he could no longer see who was calling him.

This, I thought, could work out to my advantage.

It was becoming more evident that the calf was not going to get broke yet that evening, but I was wondering if WE were going to be if the whole process continued on much longer, considering medical costs and the emotional cost of me sitting and mending more blue jeans. The calf did eventually get broke to lead in time for the fair, and led very obediently in the show ring . . . without any more ripped-out jeans.

That night I walked back to the house—slightly numbed, very amazed at our son's calm work with a ferocious beast, graciously thankful that he wasn't terribly hurt, but even more respectful of all the work that 4-H and FFA kids do to be part of a livestock show at the county fair.

I also remembered an earlier fair when some young Schwaller kids had pigs in the show ring at the livestock sale. As the auctioneer (who knows our family well) prepared the prospective buyers for bidding on this pen of pigs that belonged to our other son, he joked with the crowd saying, "Yes siree— those hogs are broke to lead, too!"

Now *that* would truly be something that mothers should not see. Except this time I would know that before I foolishly sat down to watch the show without nitroglycerine pills and an airsick bag.

This column by Karen Schwaller first
appeared in *Farm News*.

THE FARMER'S CAP

Ladies, don't lie to me now. I know you've done it. I'VE done
it. But we'll go to our graves with the one secret that could
send us there early in the first place . . . I may have thrown
away a farm cap or two in my day as a farm wife.

It's been long enough now that I have forgotten which caps I
may have tossed out to pasture. The truth is, if I don't recognize
them and they look like they've been squished into a vacuum-
sealed package that might have gone on the Apollo 13 mission,
then would they even notice if one just found its way into the
garbage bag on trash burning day? The answer is . . . of course
they would notice!

The farmer has a special connection to that which, well,
connects to his head. If women have a "thing" for shoes, then
farmers certainly have that same "thing" for caps. My dad had
hundreds of them—but he always wore the same grease-soaked
one or two; and he was the only man I ever knew who wore his
caps with the bill turned up. It looked as natural as could be on
him, since that's the only way I ever saw him wear one.

Like excuses for not dusting, farm caps are a dime a dozen,
and farmers will never pass up a new cap. They will probably also
never use most of them.

"Some of them are too cool not to have," I've been told by one
of my sons.

Not that long ago, I had grown tired of our guys' collection of
caps that were overtaking our porch and basement. I hadn't even
seen these caps on any of the guys for months—possibly years. I
made the executive decision to get rid of some, and I got a

garbage sack and began stuffing hats into it as I rejoiced silently, thinking about how we would now have an additional eight hundred or a thousand square feet in the house to use for other more useful things.

When I had finished gathering the caps and had tied the bag shut, I was halfway across the room in the basement on my way to the stairs to take them up to the attic, when my husband came into the house. Knowing that I would be paying apartment rent if he knew I was planning to eventually dispose of those sacred head pieces, I immediately did an about face and stuffed them into a busy corner before he actually got to the basement.

A few weeks later I seized an opportunity to get them to the attic without him seeing . . . relishing the fact that I at least got the caps out of plain sight for the time being. After some time had passed, my husband asked, "Where are all those caps that were over there?"

("Nerts!",I thought to myself.)

But I said calmly, "They're in the attic. Why?"

Incredulously, he wanted to know why they were up there, reasoning, "Well, we can't wear them if they're up there. Get them back down here so we can wear them."

He was standing up for farmers against their wives everywhere. Lucky for me I hadn't burned the caps right away; I would've probably been paying my own apartment rent and child support as well.

I have to say, though, that the farm cap can truly be a useful accessory. I'm told it makes a good holder for parts when you don't have anything else handy; it's a sweat catcher, cobweb duster, waver-downer of people, and was probably the original sun blocker before companies made billions with their rub-on kind. It's a holder of baby kittens, can make a little kid feel mighty big just by wearing one, and can even be used to hide underwear when blue jeans malfunction in front of mixed company. It can be part of a show of fatigue when removed and followed with a head scratch. It can also be a sign of respect to God or to someone of the opposite gender when it is removed in their presence.

Some days of the old west still live on in the modern day farmer's cap.

My most vivid memory of the use of the farmer's cap was a few years ago when, in an act of chivalry, my husband once used it to swat a fly that was on my back. (At least that's what he *told* me, anyway.) I don't know if he got the fly, but the plastic adjustor on the back of the cap certainly swatted me very effectively.

Good thing he had his cap on as he drove, to shield the glare that was coming from inside the car. Yes, farm caps are useful, indeed. For many reasons.

This column by Karen Schwaller first
appeared in *Farm News*.

FIELD MISTAKE TESTS MARRIAGE'S STRENGTH

I believe there are times when a "farm marriage" holds together only because of the bond of super glue.

Circumstances surrounding life on the farm may make the marriage appear to be stressed, much like the corn we see in the fields some years. But it seems there's always something that holds the pieces together—much like the way 25 years of dried jam and Christmas cutout cookie dough holds the two halves together in our sagging kitchen table.

Marital stress comes in many forms for the farm couple. Usually it comes in the form of too much rain or lack of it; low farm prices; too much work and a lack of time; or in one case for us, willingness with a lack of brain power behind it.

When my husband—anxious to get started planting soybeans—asked me once if I would run the field cultivator for the day, I looked at it as a chance to do something different. The only thing that made me nervous was the fact that I'd only spent a total of five-and-a-half minutes in the tractor I would be operating—an International 1066—and even so, I had to have help starting it.

Perhaps that should have been our first clue that field work and my being at the helm may not necessarily be a good combination.

I got a two-round lesson on how to field cultivate, and was left on my own to synchronize everything. I decided that I'd enjoy field cultivating a lot more if our field was six rows side by about thirty miles long, to avoid all that obnoxious turning at the end of each round. As a former drummer (and now an arm-chair drummer), I found it surprisingly complicated to know exactly when which appendage should be doing which job when the fenceline came to greet the tractor.

"You'll catch on eventually," my husband said as he left, trying to lend support.

It was of little comfort.

Two educational hours into it, I was getting it down. Then came the words that would change the day. "When you get done, go completely around (the field) three times to cover up any tracks," my husband said.

Feeling more confident, I later began my three-round trek around the field, He was disking in front of me. He turned at the edge of the bean field. I kept going on ahead with the field cultivator.

"Hmm," I thought. "This is getting a lot easier now that I've done it awhile."

I stayed close to the fenceline, made probably my best turn of the day on the corner and started going up the other side of the field. It wasn't until I was two-thirds of the way up that side of the field that I noticed my husband right behind me with the disk, waving his arms frantically.

I stopped the tractor, wondering what he could possibly want in that much of a hurry. He got out of the tractor behind me, clearly upset about something. As I opened the door on my tractor, he shouted, "What are you doing?!"

"What!"" I replied, demanding to know what I was doing wrong.

"You're tearing out corn!" he retorted angrily.

Then came the stinger—he said that one of our (then) five-year-old sons was the one who noticed it.

"But you said to go completely around the field when I got done," I meekly tried to reason.

"Around the *bean* field!" he said, driving the point home.

It had been a long time since I'd had that kind of sick feeling in the pit of my stomach. I tore out corn—which was not up yet, but which I surely must have known subconsciously had already been planted. And then a five-year-old knew that I was somewhere with the field cultivator that I shouldn't have been.

To complicate matters, I spent some time in town getting parts for his vintage 190 Allis Chalmers he was driving, which would not work after the chase scene in the field, which overworked such an old and tired machine

Settling back into our tractors later when things started to look up again, our other (then) five-year-old set the tone.

"Mommy, this time don't drive in the corn," he gently warned as he climbed into the tractor cab next to me.

Great.

The super glue came later on that day when calmness prevailed, and he told me that he'd once done much the same thing a few years ago as a hired man. There was no guilt trip, no silent treatment—although it surely was a good thing that we were in separate tractors for a while after it all happened. No marriage could withstand any amount of immediate togetherness after that kind of handiwork.

The next week, the prolonged cold weather had forced several area farmers to tear up corn so they could replant, including the farmer my husband worked for at that time.

"He could have had that done already if he had me on the payroll," I smirked.

And finally we could laugh about it all. Of all the things to be trendy about.

This column by Karen Schwaller first appeared
in the *Sioux City Journal.*

FRUSTRATION, AND CULTIVATING WISDOM

Though the days of cultivating our crops have been gulped up and replaced by sprayers, I was recently recalling a conversation I had with one of our neighborhood farm wives. I had been lamenting over something that had irritated me while I was disking one day, when she giggled and shook her head.

"I think a mistake shows there," she said, identifying my agreement to learn how to operate a tractor, let alone educate myself on the how-to's of spring tillage.

If you live on a farm, you know how hard it is to get help—or to pay for help. And it's not like just anyone knows how to drive a tractor, and can just start in. At least I had the tractor figured out, which prompted my husband one day out of desperation to ask me if I could learn how to cultivate.

No earthquake could hold a candle to the way my knees began to shake. I had disked before, but now there were actually things growing above the ground that I had to keep alive while I killed the weeds next to them. It was a frightening thought . . . perhaps for both of us.

Aside from the infamous neck pain associated with cultivating, I decided it couldn't be that hard, since farmers have been teaching their children how to cultivate since the invention of children—so I agreed to try it. How hard could it be, really?

The only bit if wisdom I knew about it before hand was from our local co-op manager who once told me (as he snickered) that, "If you see someone out cultivating and you wave at them and they wave back, it's the kid who's in the tractor and not the dad."

So at least I knew I had to look at the rows behind me and the rows in front of me, and not at the cars going by.

My husband cultivated for a couple of rounds, explaining what was what, then he offered me his chair. (Is it just me, or do we often witness them doing such gentlemanly things *outside* of a tractor cab??)

I assumed the command post after an official briefing, and we started down the rows. First, I couldn't keep the cultivator on the row. I was used to looking ahead at where I was going, not looking behind to see where I had been. And I certainly was not used to doing both at the same time, at least not so *much.*

"You're too close to this row—you better get over," he instructed gently. So I did.

"Now you're runnin' over the corn in front of you—move it over a little," he said in a little more concerned voice. So I moved it over, and then I was too close in the back again. After several tries at getting that down, exchanging some stress-related sarcasm, and administering a little bit of 'cultivator blight' here and there, I felt like I was finally getting it. But I'm sure the stress barometer inside of me was off the charts.

It probably was for my husband as well. He had to have decided after all I was doing wrong that it would be easier to train a monkey how to operate a tractor and cultivator. On the other hand, I was somewhat surprised that I had such trouble with it, since mothers should be meant for this job . . . what with the eyes we tell our kids that we have in the back of our heads.

I had just gotten to where I thought I might be able to do this job if I drove really slow and carefully, when my husband uttered the words that frightened me the most: "If you're gonna do a decent job, you have to go a little faster than this."

My eyes resembled cartoon "spinning eyes" when I heard this; was he serious? I had to go faster?? I took a deep breath and pushed the throttle ahead. Then it came: "You're too far over on this row here, move it over a little," he pointed out with an obvious running-out-of-patience voice that he was trying to disguise.

"Well, I'm *trying!*" I shot back. At that time of major frustration, I decided the pain in my neck from cultivating was sitting next to me in the cab.

"I know you're trying, but you really have to pay attention," he said, feeling the knot in his stomach tighten at the thought of leaving me there for the afternoon while he went to work in town.

I cultivated until mid-evening. It did get a little easier the more I did it, but I was glad to be done. I dialed up my husband at work to let him know that he could actually eat his supper on his lunch hour, instead of eating antacid tablets as a meal replacement. I'd gotten farther along in the field than either of us thought I would, with only a small spot or two of cultivator blight. The result was a nervous laugh, and a relief-filled and sincere, "Thanks, dear. That really helps out. Was there a lot of traffic by there today?" he inquired.

("A trap!" I thought to myself, thinking he was probably more nervous thinking that other people thought it was him out there looking like an obvious novice.)

"I don't know," I said. "I was watching the rows."

"Good job," he happily replied.

I never did tell him that I had already been given that little bit of cultivating wisdom from our local co-op manager.

This column by Karen Schwaller first
appeared in Farm News.

GRANDPA'S TRACTOR

I t was a familiar place; more familiar to some than to others. I lived there for my first eighteen years, but my parents had lived there for more than fifty years. On this day, pickup trucks lined the gravel road. I could smell the aroma from the lunch wagon. I could see people in bib overalls and greasy jeans milling about. I could hear the hiss of a John Deere Model A being started as well as the starting rumble of the other tractors lined up in the yard.

It was the day of my parents' farm sale.

Farm sale day is a day unlike any other in the life of a farmer and his family. A rite of passage, painful as it may be. My family traveled to the Remsen-Kingsley area to be part of a day that held the possibility of great things for our two boys. They had saved money all summer, and wanted nothing more than to get one of Grandpa's tractors.

For my dad, going to farm sales was something he had done often in his seventy-four years. But this sale was his, and his sorrow showed the night before the sale as his family gathered to look around the farm and share stories, laughter and tears. A farmer becomes one with the land and the work it takes. Letting go of those things used each day was so hard. The place had once been a thriving farm with lots of kids and lots of work to be done. But on that night a lifetime of sweat and grit was lined up and ready to be sold to the highest bidder.

Before the crowd arrived and the hum of the auctioneer began, my dad and I walked around the items lined up all around the yard. I wondered how he ever used all that stuff, as he gazed at it through misty, nostalgic eyes, remembering, and wondering how fifty years of farming could have possibly gone by so quickly.

He bent over to show me an item, and as he did one of his tears splashed onto it. I felt a lump in my throat, and when the auctioneer began, I realized it was all really happening.

It was quite a feeling at first, seeing three of my four brothers on the flat racks with the auctioneer, holding up parts of their own farm memories for the bidders to see, then handing things over to new owners. They had worked hard with our dad, with all of it, and they had also worked hard to get it ready to sell.

Finally it was time to sell the farm equipment. Our sons had stomachaches, worried that there were plenty of other bidders out there who had more money than they. But no other bidders had more desire to own one of Grandpa's tractors than those two boys on that day.

The first tractor, a John Deere A, sold to my oldest brother.

I told him, "It's really cool you got that tractor."

As he replied, "Well, it's been here fifty years," he began to choke up.

It used to amaze me, as a kid, to watch Dad and my brothers start that tractor. I'd thought it positively mystifying to see them turn the flywheel by hand to get it started.

Other tractors and equipment sold, including an older Honda motorcycle that one of our sons purchased. Soon it was time to sell the tractor our boys wanted, an Oliver 1750, the only tractor that my father had ever bought brand new. Grandpa Art's farm was the only home that tractor had ever known.

The boys had set their top price and stood nervously beside their dad as he did the bidding for them. As the bidding went on, they soon neared their top-end price. They bid yet another time and another. Soon their dad could see it would go too far over their price, and shook his head sadly as he looked at the boys. He knew how much they wanted that tractor.

I felt their disappointment. It showed on their faces, and probably on my own. The bidding continued, but then, as if a miracle had occurred, the man who was bidding against our sons somehow figured out that grandsons were bidding on the tractor, and he backed off.

The auctioneer cried, "Sold!" as he had so many times that day, then came over and shook our sons' hands, congratulating them on becoming the proud new owners of one of Grandpa Art's most beloved tractors.

The boys were overcome with joy, as were many there in that moment. Tears flowed, by family members and friends of all ages. The auctioneer later told me he had to look away because he was afraid he would start crying, too. Many hands clapped, sharing in our happiness and relief, and cheers went out for a tractor that went to two young farmers who had fallen in love with it, simply because it was one of their grandpa's tractors.

The tractor was loaded up on a trailer and taken to its new home, with yellow and black streamers, placed on it by our sons' very happy aunts, billowing from it.

The next night the boys and I sat down to e-mail my youngest brother in Arkansas to let him know they had purchased Grandpa's tractor. My husband said, "Why don't you tell the rest of the story, guys?"

Looking sheepishly at me, one of them said, "We broke the headlight out on the motorcycle."

I knew he was speaking of the older Honda they had just bought at the auction. "How did that happen already?" I inquired.

After a pause, he replied, "I hit the 1750. We're not used to the throttle yet."

It felt really good to laugh.

This column by Karen Schwaller first
appeared in *Farm News*.

GARDENING AND HOME CANNING

I t can cause quite a calamity, you know. Gardening, that is. I haven't invested my time and energies into that for a while now, but I used to do it quite religiously when our children were growing up. It all began as soon as that first seed hit the soil in the spring, and it trudged on long after the leaves were crunchy under our feet as we carried our produce in for another batch of homemade misery. It was kind of a love-hate thing, and sometimes I just wasn't in the mood.

I first had to master the art of gardening if I was to assure myself a lifetime full of home-canning fables I could refer to if I ever felt the desire to get rid of any unwanted company. I've learned many things among the rows and vines over the years. They include:

1) You plant only one hill of squash if you want occasional visits from the neighbors; two or more hills planted in the spring, and they'll see you this winter. No one wants that much squash in their trunk . . . and everyone knows there's no such thing as a zucchini crop failure.

2) Pigweeds have more lives than Evel Knievel.

3) Tomato plants get the award for the most obnoxious smelling plants in the northern hemisphere.

4) A bowl full of garden fresh cut-up onions are much easier to be around after they've been put in the dehydrator.

5) If you don't care if something grows, it will. The things you really want to grow will be eaten off by transient varmints and microscopic microorganisms.

6) Necessary weeding comes shortly before your hands and nails will be in public view, just in time for people to think you've just degreased a motor.

I also learned over the years that there are many different methods for harvesting garden goodies. While many families utilized the parent-and-kid approach, I usually preferred the "mom alone" method when I first began to harvest vegetables to preserve. Since our (then) very young children were eager to help pick from the vines, doing it myself rendered my garden useful for yet another picking . . . or, for that matter, for another day's growth.

And while I usually didn't practice the FITA (Fanny in the air) method (for visual reasons), a new strawberry patch in the garden one year necessitated a change in methods for me. I learned that if you're going to get all those berries, you have to pick 'em that way. I'm not a fan of the way it looks—a S.W.A.T. team could have practiced on my backside in all the times I had it sticking up in the air picking those darn strawberries. If you've ever been saved by their sharp-shooting skills, you could probably thank me.

Having an attractive garden can also be a trick. At our house, it used to be done with mowers.

We have mowers with four wheels and some with four legs. And I've learned that replanting a garden two or three times because of a hungry rabbit or a wandering sheep can turn an otherwise law-abiding citizen into a rock-toting, Elmer Fudd type with a watchful eye and a Super Soaker ready at all times. I now know why the *Winnie the Pooh* character "Rabbit" is always so hyper.

I once went to visit one of our neighbor ladies who shared quite a bit of her wisdom with me. I told her that I had canned some green beans that week, and she said to me, "This year I went to the grocery store and did my canning—they had all their vegetables really cheap last week and I stocked up."

If only I had thought of that.

Oh, we "turnip" our noses at the thought of all that work, but we "relish" the things we've harvested, even if we've gotten ourselves into a "jam" a time or two getting it all done. And when we feel "beet" afterwards, and we see that our garden did amount to a "hill of beans," we can sit back in "peas" and quiet, knowing that our gardening tenacity can't be "squashed" because the proof is taking up all of our counter space.

As for my own gardening and home-canning philosophy, it goes like this: "Home canning is kind of like having children. Whether you planned to do it or not, it helps if you're in the mood."

Well, it goes something like that, anyway.

This column by Karen Schwaller first appeared
in the *Sioux City Journal.*

THE KITCHEN TABLE INCIDENT

I've been gullible in my life on many occasions—from planning picnics based on the weather forecast, right down to that "for better, for worse" part in our wedding vows.

(That can be an especially cruel one the longer harvest season drags out and the less sleep your farmer husband gets. I'm hoping that a show of hands would indicate that I'm not the only one in that boat.)

But, I have never been taken so much the fool as I was by our own kids one evening a few years ago. Let me tell you the story.

It began when our kids (ages eleven, nine and nine) decided that they were too cool to be friends with each other. All of a sudden, fights broke out over the simplest of things—whose turn it was to feed which pen of pigs, how they were to be fed and how long it should take to feed them. In the time they spent fighting, the job could have been long finished.

My husband and I, sick and tired of all the bickering going on (and tired of the children's fighting as well!) intervened, showing them that if they would just work together, they could get a lot done in a short time.

One evening, I returned home from work to find the kids were already doing chores, and coming up to tell me how much they had gotten done.

"That's awesome, guys!" I said, praising them for getting things done. "I'll be out to help you in a few minutes." I went inside, put my things on the kitchen table and changed into my chore clothes.

When I got outside, I kept telling them how good of a feeling it was to see that they could work together and get everything done without the cloak of darkness governing anything we had to do outside. I used my psychology to the max: *"Praise them when they do something right."* And boy did I do that.

After chores were done, I went inside with a light heart to start supper. When I entered the kitchen that second time, I thought the table looked different—more saggy than usual. The fact of the matter is that our table had been held together for the past 15 years by the remains of cut out cookie goop, dried jelly and spilled milk. But even this looked suspicious.

I took my purse, camera bag and shoulder brief case off of the table and removed the tablecloth, only to discover that the table was broken. The support boards underneath the table were busted.

And so were they.

Since they weren't in the house to witness my head ready to explode, I removed everything from the table and set the table for supper, everything sliding towards the center of the table where it was broken. That way they knew that I knew why they had been working together so well. That's how we (quietly) ate our supper that night.

Eventually two of the three ratted out their brother, but not completely.

"He just leaned on it like this and it broke," our daughter said, placing her elbows on the table to show us that he had just carefully placed his arms on the table and miraculously, the table broke.

I must have had tire tracks on my forehead from when I fell off the turnip truck.

My husband had put in a long day in the field, and I laid the news on him before he got home so he wouldn't have the same shock I had upon seeing it. When he got home, he sawed a board to place as a prop under the table to get us by for the next twenty years, I suspected. If the truth were known, I dreamed of a sag-free table for years, but didn't think I'd get it this way.

Perhaps it would be dangerous for me to dream of a sag-free midsection.

Not long after that, my husband and I had a meeting to attend. We toyed with the idea of letting the kids stay home by themselves for a couple of hours. Unbelievably, we decided to do just that, and thought the whole time about what else was going to be broken.

When we returned home, they met us at the door, much like they did on that infamous night of the table breaking incident.

The hair on my neck stood on end.

When we went on the tour, we saw that the porch and basement, and the basement steps—had all been cleaned and swept, all the toilets and sinks had been cleaned, the dishes were done and two loads of laundry had been done.

Homework was finished, their showers were taken, and their teeth were brushed.

"Man," I said nervously. "You guys can get a lot done when you work together like this."

I still haven't had the nerve to go up and look in the attic yet.

Ignorance really is bliss.

This column by Karen Schwaller first
appeared in *Farm News*.

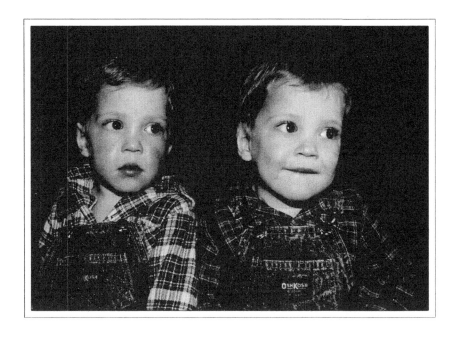

GROWING PAINS FOR YOUNG AND OLD

I'm just taking a guess here, but I'm thinking that if we had to grow up again, we probably would opt not to go through it another time.

Some of us still hadn't had it nailed down in our thirty-something years. Perhaps it is somewhat similar to that old adage that, "Good things come to those who wait."

I'm certain my mother wonders if she'll ever see the fruits of her labors in her lifetime, as I think about the wise person who once wrote that, "Mothers help build cathedrals that they may never see finished."

The lessons learned as we grow up are tough ones—there's just no two ways about it. Take our children's behavior during an outbreak of severe weather once when they were very young.

The weather forecasters gave us fair warning that the storm was going to hit, and we could see that it was going to happen. And so could our daughter. In just nine years she had gotten weather worrying down to an art.

"I don't like this . . . My stomach hurts . . . I'm getting a headache," she would say, with great fear in the delivery of those worrisome statements.

Finally, after it was decided to descend into the basement, her emotions came to a head and she burst into a fireball of frustrated tears. "Mom, how can you stay so calm?!" she demanded tearfully.

After we talked about how worrying doesn't stop the wind from blowing or the rain from coming down, we entered the basement bedroom to hang out for a while. Our two boys were already down there, bathed in fear and hunkering down for the storm—covers up to their chins and shaking like two scared little peas in a pod.

"What's happenin' down here, guys?" I asked, trying to keep the mood light while the thunder rattled our windows and the lights flickered off and on for the dozenth time.

I failed miserably at lightening the already thick atmosphere.

"Mom?" one of them asked with a quivering voice. "I'm scared. I want to live past first grade."

The tip of my tongue was sore for days from biting it to keep from laughing. It was so sweet and innocent—and fear-riddled. I was certain I would think of it every time we had such a storm to endure after that.

Another kind of growing pain occurred a short time after that when we visited my husband's aging grandfather in a nursing home.

It had been a long time since we'd made the time to visit him, and knew that he may not be the same as we remembered him.

We told the kids beforehand that Grandpa Joe may not remember us, but that it was one of the things that happen when people get older. We discussed it a little more, and we all went in with our smiles turned on.

When we got into his room, Grandpa Joe did not know any of us, and said so. It was hard to visit about much of anything since he didn't know who we were, then eventually it was time to say good-bye. We did so, then quietly left.

It was a growing pain for every age that afternoon as we emerged from the nursing home, and headed to our car. Our daughter was fighting back her tears, hurt that a man she had loved as much as her Grandpa Joe now didn't know who she was. It's hard to understand about this lesson in life when you're nine years old.

Or older.

We all shared a few tears over what once was and would never be again; talked about it a little more, and went on with the rest of our day. It was apparent that none of us would be the same after seeing and knowing that such a part of our heritage was now tucked away in an old man's memories, never to be unlocked again.

What was left to do after the silence of sorrow broke was to think of a happy or funny thing we remembered about Grandpa Joe.

We laughed through misty eyes as my husband told about the time when he was in high school, and Grandpa (and Grandma) Joe had come to visit them. Our local Mexican restaurant is quite a calling card for many around the area, and he and his sister had brought home some tacos for supper that night.

Grandpa Joe, being a grain and livestock farmer at heart (at one time, farming with horses), and obviously being more of a "meat-and-potatoes guy" than a taco man, observed the situation and plainly uttered, "I've cleaned up better looking messes than that."

Laughter is great, isn't it? Especially when we can do it after we've suffered through the never-ending pains that growing up requires—no matter how old we are when that growing up occurs.

This column by Karen Schwaller first
appeared in *Farm News*.

THE BARNYARD GATE

There's something inherently unnatural about seeing a cow run past your living room window.
At least we live in the country, so it might seem a little more natural there than it would be if we lived in town and witnessed that same kind of farmyard calamity.

We've had tractors, hay racks and bale elevators parked up by the house from time to time as household projects came to the front burner—but enough about my housecleaning habits. That being said, even those things by the house don't seem as out of place or worrisome as a cow on a home-stretch sprint past the windows that you've just cleaned.

You never know what's going to come out the back end of that cow—whether she's nearing calving time or just needs to use the restroom.

I don't care who they are—cows, sheep, pigs, goats—they can sense an open gate with more intuitive prowess than a gypsy fortune-teller. It's their job to act all contented, letting the farmer think they can be trusted, then as soon as they hear a chain rattling, take off like they're at the Kennedy Space Center . . . or as if they're Liz Taylor running after her next husband.

I've uttered the phrase to a few people, and I think it holds true for farm babies as well as humans. Bill Cosby once said that ". . . babies should be sued for false advertising, because nobody ever wanted a fourteen-year-old." (Okay, so we DO want our 14-year-olds, but you know what he was saying . . .)

I think we could make that a crossover statement into barnyard animals as well. They're so dang cute as little babies—

71

even pigs. But have you ever crossed a sow when she's on a mission? Or tried to carry a couple of pails of corn across a yard full of sheep?

You're either out of the way, or someone will pour maple syrup on you the next morning because you'll be breakfast material. They'll flatten you and won't even work up a good sweat doing it. Then they'll mock you by looking back and slowing their pace to a trot, watching us wave our arms and catch up to them.

All the nerve.

They all start out so cute and loveable, and then grow up to be sly, cunning and proud of the way they can make us humans look like we belong in the kiddie pool of life. Have you ever tried to chase a hog into an open gate or doorway? You might as well just get the nitro-glycerin pills out before you even start. They do love to test our athletic prowess, and our will to not become vegetarians as they run past that open gate or door for the 156th time.

After all, it's their job to see if we're worth the sausage. It's not like they contribute to the breakfast meal like chickens do. As they say—all give some, some give all. I guess hogs just want to make sure we're worth it first.

Operating the barnyard gate is a terrible post if you're the kid or the wife of a farmer when things aren't going well. It's all fine and dandy until the whole herd of "whatevers" think they have heard someone sound the retreat, and they all come bolting toward the gate with the ferocity of a locomotive with no one in the conductor's seat. If you can get the gate locked in time, great. If not, you're either breakfast material again, or you're hearing the Lord's name in vain from a voice that's above you, but certainly not His. And even if the gate got locked in time, it's now the shape of a crescent moon and you're a hundred yards away to avoid injury or death.

Who says we can't run like we did in high school track?

I recently saw a cow running past our living room window. It was quite striking, actually, with the black cow against the red of the buildings and the white of the snow all around. Once again, it's all fine and dandy until you see people running behind with their arms waving. Somehow it takes away from the serenity of the scene, even if the cow isn't supposed to be out. There always has to be a farmer running behind.

It seems somehow unfair for farm animals to be chased by humans—four legs against two. Even the government would complain about that gross injustice, I think.

I once read something that said, "Live like someone left the gate open."

Around here, the gates really do get left open, and living here then is not a pleasant experience. It's obvious that the person who invented that saying never lived on a farm.

Many I know live like someone left the barn door open . . . only the barn door isn't on the barn. I guess there will always be a need for a farm mom or wife, if only to help us get dressed, and make sure all barn doors are closed when the day begins.

This column by Karen Schwaller first
appeared in *Farm News*.

LEAVING THE COWS

Agricultural roots run deep.

As I write this, our community will say its final farewell to an old farmer. A giant of a man—not in physical stature, but of character. He was a quiet and hardworking man who stayed busy enough taking care of his own business that he didn't have time to worry about anyone else's. He was a kind and gentle man who loved his family and the work that he was called to do in this life—raising the food that feeds the world.

But to him, it was more than food for the world. It was who he was, and his identity as a farmer ran parallel to the love he had for his vocation, but especially for his milk cows.

That love of farming and of milking the cows ran just as deep for his wife. They worked together for all of the sixty-five years they were married. Much of their time together was spent working together on the farm, but some of their favorite time was spent in the milking barn.

Devoted to their lives on the farm, they rarely ever left other than to haul commodities to the elevator or run a few errands in town. So when their son announced that he was to be married away from their hometown, it meant that they would need to spend a few days away to attend the wedding. But it also meant they would be away from their milk cows—that they protected almost as much as their own children.

It also meant they would have to trust someone with their care, but whom? It was the first time in a quarter of a century that they would miss a milking.

Certainly it had taken them hours of thought to decide who they would leave their beloved cows with, but apparently my husband had made the cut. And so the date was set for my husband to come over and get the how-tos from them for doing their chores.

There were various chores, but when they entered the milking barn together, my husband could plainly see that it wasn't just about milking the cows—it was about the relationships that these people had established with those four-legged and gentle beasts.

As they walked around, the man's wife showed him where all of the equipment was, and then she introduced my husband to each of the cows in their small herd. "This one likes to be scratched under the chin," she said as she showed him exactly where. ". . . and this one likes just a little extra slab of hay . . . and this one's name is (whatever)."

Her quiet husband followed behind, smiling and winking at my husband as she laid out the specifics about every cow in the barn. He didn't have much to say about it, except to lovingly suggest to her that she might be telling my husband a little more than he really needed to know. (Followed by that characteristic and peaceful smile and wink.)

It was clearly going to be hard for them to leave for those few days, but it was going to be the most personal experience of milking cows that my husband would ever have—given that responsibility by two people who could only be taken away from their cows by such an event as the wedding of one of their children.

My husband learned something in that time as well. He decided that if reincarnation was true, he would want to come back to earth as one of their cows, because he could see by their gentle nature, how well they were cared for. (That may or may not say something about the way I had cared for my husband; names can be changed to protect the innocent.) He could see that those cows not only were loved, but felt loved. They each produced far more milk than he could have ever imagined.

It was a sad day a few years later when they decided they were no longer able to continue milking, and the cows left the farm. Farewells were said between man and beast, and quiet tears followed.

Those quiet tears will flow again today as we take this wonderful man to his final place of rest. He will return to the land he loved so much, to be part of it in a different—and perhaps, more personal—way.

Agricultural roots run deep. And thank God they do, for the sake of the next generation—who will also find themselves someday resting in the land they have loved. That kind and depth of love could only be handed down to them by their brothers in agriculture—just like the one we remember today.

This column by Karen Schwaller first
appeared in *Farm News*.

HITTING THE ROAD

It was getting to the point where the kids were able to identify with the things their dad said more than I was. They could talk about the places he—and they—had been, and I just sat there and got whiplash from following their conversations, looking from one person to another, as their fables and tales went back and forth. After all, they'd experienced many travels together.

Finally, the day came when I was able to slip inside the clique. I had a day off on the same day my husband had a load of cattle to haul to Omaha. The date was made and I was off to meet my husband as soon as the yellow school bus swallowed our children and left our driveway.

It's hard to explain—why it's exciting to spend the day in a cubicle, following a never-ending strip of concrete, dodging D.O.T. vehicles and cow droppings, and climbing half the height of a redwood forest tree to get into and out of the truck. But the sheer appeal of it all finally beckoned me to take the passenger seat and experience the open road, at least as open as it gets when you have to be back to meet the kids after school.

Actually, it was kind of nice. With the hectic pace we keep up, it had been a long time since one of us could talk to the other for more than a few minutes without one of us hearing snoring from the other before we were finished with a story.

But the truth of the matter was that it had been a long time since we had any time to talk without stopping to referee the kids' squabbles, hear about their day, or run with a first aid rag somewhere around the farmyard. This was our time, and we were actually looking forward to it.

I met my husband at a farm west of Milford where he was loading cattle. I decided to get our lunch box (more commonly referred to around here as a "nose bag") into the truck, and get myself situated. I walked the length of the trailer and was almost up to the cab before I heard things leaking out of the loaded pot trailer behind me.

Immediately I realized I had already lucked out without even knowing it. I learned then and there that you walk the length of a loaded trailer from the distance of a few feet out, instead of as if you were approaching your car from behind. After all, it's not like being grossed out when a bird finds you from up above. (Yeesh.)

As I waited inside the truck for my husband, I could hear a phone ringing. I looked atop of the dash and saw a phone, but that one wasn't ringing. Finally, the ringing phone that was somewhere in the cab, stopped. Relieved, I settled in for the drive. Then the phone I did see began to ring. Having little or no experience with cell phones at that time, I fumbled with it, trying to figure out which button to push. Finally, I pushed a button and promptly cut the caller off. I put the phone back, only to have it ring again. This time we made connections and I gave my husband the message it took the caller three tries to send.

As my sweaty husband entered the truck and we began the journey to Omaha, I was feeling like I should have brought my parka on that chilly fall morning. My attempts to maintain a normal body temperature were met with, "Wow—are you warm enough yet?" as the sweat beads gathered on his forehead. He told me it would be my full time job to run the heater control in the truck, and he was right. It went back and forth more times than Dennis Rodman and the NBA officials. I also didn't want to look completely inept as I went to roll down my window, but after a while I was forced to ask about the window crank. My husband showed me the electric switch on the panel that controlled the window. Duh.

As the trip began, habit had me lock the door on my side. When it was time to get out of the truck, I couldn't unlock the door. My husband had to fish out his pliers and give them to me so I could lift the lock.

I knew at that point that the kids were less trouble to take along on these trips.

That point was compounded a few minutes later at a truck stop we'd stopped at, when I boldly stepped into the men's room to do what the cattle were doing inside and out the side of the truck. As I closed the door and noticed the sign, I looked around quickly to see if anyone saw me. Indeed, someone had.

I could hear Charlie Brown saying, "This just isn't my day."

Finally, as we neared Omaha, my husband had to awaken me so I didn't miss the processing plant. (I must have traveled beautifully as a child—sitting in the passenger seat in trucks puts me right under.)

As it goes, the cattle got to where they were supposed to go, and we had some time to spend together (when I wasn't sleeping; I'm assuming he didn't' sleep); and I got a chance to be included in some of the conversations my husband and kids had been sharing in.

It could be awhile before he asks me to go with him again, however. It just might be easier to leave me at home.

This column by Karen Schwaller first
appeared in *Farm News*.

THE VAN DOOR INCIDENT

I need a show of hands here: how many of you have ever experienced issues with your vehicle? I'm not talking about running out of gas or needing to put in a new water pump or fuel pump. (Though the cost of those things can pump my husband up plenty.)

I'm talking about things that no one would believe if you told them; things that would make them think you were . . . well, a moron. Put your feet up and let me share a vision with you.

It all started last fall. You see, it's a responsibility I share with another farm wife to feed a tribe of eight or nine hungry men every other night as they are harvesting. I already have a full time job which takes mucho extra time in the fall as it is, so that means that between a job, a photography sideline that kicks into high gear in the fall, livestock chores, planning and cooking meals for all those guys, and laundry and dishes to keep up with, I should weigh slightly less than a cockroach on meth. What it actually does mean is that things have to go like clockwork in order for the plan to hang together each day. There's only so much room for things to go wrong—but trouble always seems to rear its ugly head.

It was your typical fall day. I had prepared a great supper for the guys in the field the evening before, so that all I had to do was pop it in the oven after work, head out to do chores, load it all up in the van and haul it out to somewhere in Nebraska or South Dakota or wherever it seemed like they were working that night.

(Ladies, let's be honest: we love our guys, but do you not tire of the job of hauling food all over North America on the "'Til the Cows Come Home" plan??)

Anyway, I was going to leave work a little early in order to make it all fit in that night. I didn't leave work quite on time, but it was still okay.

I put my things in the van, and went to close the sliding door on the driver's side. The door had been working a little hard lately, and I couldn't accomplish the task with one arm (tendonitis in the elbow.) SO, I did what any good farm wife would do—I two-armed the door to get it shut.

And that's when it happened.

The entire sliding door fell off of the side of the van. WHOA!! If I thought I was strong in anything other than smell, I would never have attempted such a feat. This was ridiculous, even for me!

Naturally, since I was in a parking lot in town, I feigned the look that says "It's cool," and looked around to see if anyone had the misfortune of seeing what had just occurred. I tried to see if I could just slip the door back into the track where it fell out. I lifted the van door, and the only thing that accomplished was to make me look ridiculous, and prove that octopi are highly underrated.

I set the door down—not thinking about how maddening it was that the door had just fallen off of the van, but at how mad I was that my plan with my great meal had been foiled . . . so to speak. It would take forever to get everything done now.

SO—I did what any responsible farm wife would do under these circumstances—I called my husband who was combining.

Following a double inquiry to ensure that he heard me correctly, the laughing began. When he could speak again, the plan was made, and I called the local body shop; luckily, they were still open yet. The guy came and got the door temporarily put back on with little to no fanfare for all of his skills in parking lot "doors-falling-off-the-side-of-vans" repairs. (Shouldn't there be some kind of music for that??)

I ordered out for supper, and when I got to the field, I handed one of my sons a Styrofoam box. He asked where the meatballs were that he had been looking forward to, so I said, "Well,"—knowing he would never believe the story—"they're going to be for supper next time because the door fell off of the side of the van after work."

It was like telling a pack of laughing hyenas once the men all flocked around and heard the story. Supper-time van door inspections were made under the lights of combines, semis and tractors hooked to grain carts. And I spent the rest of the night making supper deliveries and then going home, paranoid the entire time that the door would fly off as I was driving down the road.

I really wished that the cows had already come home by then.

This column by Karen Schwaller first
appeared in *Farm News*.

HOMEMADE SPAGHETTI SAUCE
IS OVERRATED

I'm certain that the person who said, "Children should be seen and not heard" must have been a young mother who was trying courageously to can spaghetti sauce.

One year when our daughter was at school and our boys were pre-school age, I went against my better judgment and embarked on the whole new venture of making homemade spaghetti sauce for the first time. "It's so easy," I'd hear ". . . and it tastes so much better than the stuff you can buy."

Well, making the sauce wasn't bad, but twin boys underfoot and over my head made it a most interesting experience. As a result, I have a special recipe to pass along to you. I call it, "Double Spaghetti Sauce."

Here goes:

*Begin with prepared tomatoes. Clean off the toys that got tossed into the sink of tomato-washing water. Peel a few more tomatoes. Fix a toy that the boys want to play with, then settle the fight when only one of them gets the toy. Return to the kitchen, making sure to trip over a toy horse they've left on the floor.

*Continue peeling tomatoes. Get the boys a snack. Peel tomatoes, while stopping periodically to answer them as to what kind of animal is on the animal cracker they're eating. Answer the door and entertain unexpected company. Finish peeling tomatoes and move onto green peppers, onions and garlic.

*Get a good start on the peppers, then help both boys in the bathroom, as Mother Nature has called, in duplicate. Find something for them to do, and continue with the peppers. After the twins become bored with an entire house full of toys, have them help you so they can be doing something you can be witness to in case a fight breaks out. Continue preparing peppers. Answer the phone. Settle yet another fight over a coveted wooden spoon they each want. Finish with the peppers and pick up the dinner table bench they've tipped over. Prepare onions.

*Take the knife away from one of the boys, who seemed to get a hold of one out of nowhere. Finish onions and start on garlic cloves. Pick up the dinner table bench again, put it away and lock yourself in a closet with the telephone, reserving in your name all the spaghetti sauce in stock at the local supermarket. A cold compress to the forehead will finish the recipe nicely.

Our daughter emerged from the school bus that afternoon, but would never know her real mother again after the trauma of that day. Pity . . . especially after all of the spaghetti sauce I'd wiped out of my children's hair, elbows and armpits when they were all still in high chairs yet.

I know a man who says he can't eat boughten spaghetti sauce, and that if they run out of the homemade brew at his home, he'd rather wait however long it takes to grow ripe tomatoes and have his wife wave her magic wooden spoon over them, turning them into her tantalizing spaghetti sauce.

Personally, after my exasperating experience at canning spaghetti sauce, I think the boughten stuff tastes pretty dang good.

And so does my therapist.

This column by Karen Schwaller first appeared
in the *Sioux City Journal.*

HOUSE AND CAR CLEANING

There are so many people in this world who know so much. I mean important things like that age-old trick (for women and men) about how to make your hair defy gravity by combing it straight up, or that it takes a certain amount of patience, skill and thinking like a cow in order to break a 4-H calf beginning the week before the fair.

It's great that in these days of "information at your fingertips" and running ourselves ragged to get it all done, that we can still do some things the old fashioned way—by looking to our elders for the things we *really* need to know.

Older people are like our information superhighway that actually walk and talk to us—but the difference is that they can tell us how to do something and add all that stuff that the internet doesn't. For example, a recipe can tell you that you can add squash to it, but the older, experienced cooks can tell you that your kids probably would use it to do experiments on the cat if you do; or—that being involved in the life of your grown kids is important, but that you can resemble a horse's hind-end if you are too involved. You know . . . stuff like that.

It happened one afternoon as I was in my office. The housekeeper came in with her usual feather duster and smile, pulling a vacuum behind her. Her smile in and of itself was amazing, considering she has to clean my office after (what seems like) the contents of Noah's Ark has passed through there during the course of a week.

(Noah had no idea when he built the ark, nor did I know that they would all be in MY office after they stepped off of the ark.)

But as we got to visiting in our usual way that afternoon, she just blurted something out that really got me to thinking. Well actually, it horrified me and gave me a knot in my stomach; which wasn't the worst thing, considering it was the most exercise my stomach had had in quite some time.

She ran her feather duster around the book shelves and windowsill and was laughing and chatting with me as we exchanged wisdoms about home, family and her frustration over her guess that a man must have picked out the carpet in my office because it's so hard to keep clean. And then she said it. "You know, if you look in a woman's car, her house looks just the same."

There was no warning or anything that this kind of shocking statement was coming.

"Oh man," I thought to myself, as I did the one-eyebrow-up-thing. I couldn't have been more horrified than if Madonna herself had showed up on our church step. Had this woman ever seen the inside of our car? Had she seen the inside of our house? Was she trying to tell me something that I needed to know?

This woman is really into housekeeping. I classify her in the same category as my big sister—saying that the most obvious difference between us (growing up in the same house and being taught the same housekeeping skills) is that you could eat off of her floor and not even think twice about doing so; and you could eat off of *my* floor and get full.

When my mother comes to visit, she must really wonder where she went wrong. Most times she just makes her way into the house and walks swiftly with arms outstretched, reaching for the dish soap; or she starts folding the laundry that has been in baskets in the living room since the Regan administration. My sister just leaves me a note in the dust somewhere when I'm not looking, then waits to see how long it'll take me to find it. It's great entertainment for her. I'd do the same at her house, but I'd have to bring the dust in order to do it . . . which I could probably manage.

Okay, so my housekeeping habits have tended to take a back seat to other obligations and, well, to other things I'd rather do. But now I'm feeling the pressure that I have to keep my car clean, too. How do older people know things like this??

I tend to prefer my neighbor's thinking about dusting her house. She said, "I've decided that dust is just part of my country look."

Her car probably looks like mine. Whew. Thank God I'm not the only one.

This column by Karen Schwaller first
appeared in *Farm News*.

WHY WE KNOW GOD WASN'T A FARMER

You have to wonder about some people sometimes. And then, you have to wonder about other people all of the time.

I've been a farmer's wife for twenty-five years and I wonder about myself most of the time.

I became a partner in this manic farming craze on my own free will when I married my friend under the auspices of God. And still today, I think He could have come to me in a dream as He did to St. Joseph, to tell me to take the low road out to . . . well, somewhere else, before I got in too deep for knee boots or for my own mental health.

I've decided over the past few years that farming had to have been invented by someone other than our Supreme Creator.

Otherwise, I would think that life would make a lot more sense than it does. I've come up with a list of ways in which we know that God was not a farmer.

Maybe some of them will strike you as well.

*Reason Number One: God took time to rest on the seventh day. Have you ever known a farmer to be happy sitting around the house when there are sows to vaccinate, sheep to work and crops to maintain? In most farm families, the seventh day is the day in which you work the hardest on the farm, because it's the only full day he has away from his job in town.

*Number Two: It's most likely that he didn't contact the Global Apple Growers Association in the Garden of Eden before He spoke of the scandalous fruit incident involving Adam and Eve. A simple public-relations mistake.

*Number Three: A flood was the answer to His problems. Now that's a different take.

*Number Four: He made weeds more sustainable than any other plants on earth.

*Number Five: He made planting time come in the spring, when rains can delay planting and gale-force winds can hamper or delay critical windows of opportunity for spraying . . . making farmers begin to resemble those big, black or brown beasts found largely in Alaska.

*Number Six: If He thought He made hogs intelligent, I wonder what animal He made to be well, less smart??

*Number Seven: He made only twenty-four hours in a day. How can farmers expect to get three days' work done in only twenty-four hours? And since He had no wife, God couldn't have experienced the anguish involved in cooking something at 6 p.m. for the children, and needing to keep it warm and edible to feed a hungry husband at dark-thirty (thirty minutes after dark).

*Number Eight: One word—hail.

*Number Nine: He made animals able to outrun people. What in the . . . ???

*Number Ten: He would have equipped farm wives with radar, so that when her husband points into a pen of pigs and tells her to bring *that* hog over to him, she actually knows which hog he means.

*Number Eleven: He would have designed winter more consistently, in that there would be enough snow to irrigate the soil for crops without having to spend hours moving it. After all, snow is a four-letter word to most farmers.

*Number Twelve: He would have made grease—the farmer's staple—more easily removable from hands and clothing.

*Number Thirteen: After He sent the locusts to teach Biblical people a lesson, I would think He would have done away with other insects which can do enough damage to cause farmers to take His name in vain. Perhaps only a hollow victory.

As you can see, there are many things which God could have done differently to make the life of farmers and their families easier, but in an amazing stroke of genius, He made farm wives able to work ground after only a single round's worth of instructions in the field, before her farmer husband rushes off to begin the next pressing project. And more amazingly, He made the farm wife loyal, understanding and ready to drop everything when her help is needed in the fields or out in the stock yards.

He gave farmers the guts to gamble with all they have on another years' crop. He gave them enough fire to get the job done no matter what the conditions, yet made them gentle and compassionate enough to want to nurture the land and all who live there.

He gives them enough trials to bear so that they remain humble servants of the land, and enough success to make them want to do it all over again next year. And He gave them a sense of great being—knowing that their livelihood and future lie directly in His hands.

What more is there to understand about the way God created farming . . . and farmers?

This column by Karen Schwaller first
appeared in *Farm News*.

HOW DO YOU KNOW IF YOU'RE A FARM WIFE?

Sooner or later, every farm wife begins to feel like one. She is often seen in the shadow of her husband, yet she manages to find the gall to work side by side with him on projects that lead them through everything from nailing tin onto barn roofs, to burrowing through the aromatic piles which accumulate underneath the farrowing crates. She may be handling the manure scraper in one hand while leafing through a job description of the farm wife with the other hand . . . wondering if these tasks are in the fine print, or if she is pitching out some of her husband's own brand of philosophy at the end of the scraper.

There are signs that can tell you if you are a true farm wife. Beware of the ones to which you find a chilling similarity. You may be a farm wife if:

1) You're still waiting to see who shot J. R. Ewing because that was the last time you had the time to watch television.

2) Seed corn numbers begin to make as much sense to you as they do to your husband.

3) Buying a new pair of jeans for your husband is a mixed-emotion thing. You can finally throw away that pair of mended jeans with 12 or 13 patches, happy to not have to sew on them anymore. But at the same time, you're disgusted that all that work will now be landfill (or air pollution), and you're

just as disgusted that you will have to do that much work to the pair you just bought before they, too, can be retired.

4) Family planning discussions make it known that birthday parties for any forthcoming children will probably be winter ones, since you may find yourself in the delivery room by yourself during any given spring, summer or fall month if your husband decides it's time to plant or harvest the crop, or if there is hay to bale.

5) You're walking through the living room and get yelled at by a seed corn-capped, implement-laden five-year-old saying, "You're walking on my corn field!"

6) Your clean laundry on the clothes line smells like livestock if the wind is right (or wrong) on manure hauling day, or if it's dirtier than it was before you washed it because of those obnoxious, wafting clouds of gravel road dust.

7) Everything else you loathe pales in comparison to the thought of mending a pair of insulated coveralls with a hole in the pliers pocket.

8) The only sewing machine needles in your possession are the heavier ones that will plow through several layers of denim . . . or the pliers pocket on a pair of insulated coveralls.

9) If every family outing becomes a business trip, taking you past every implement dealer on the way to wherever you're going. And that's even if you're not really looking for anything.

10) If you still (on occasion) judge the worthiness of various farm publications by what's on the recipe page.

If any or all of these episodes sound familiar to you, don't panic and head to your nearest mental health facility. You're probably not crazy, but sometimes it helps to be reassured by a professional that you still have all your marbles, even if they may not be packed as tightly now as they may have been at one time.

Take the husband-helping ritual. "When I go like this, (he makes a hand gesture) it means to do (this). When I go like this, (he makes another hand gesture) it means to do (that)," he says.

Sounds easy. Then when things get going, he makes some unexplained gesture which makes complete nonsense to the farm wife. She doesn't have a clue what she's supposed to do to keep the project going and to keep from getting yelled at, so she punts.

If the decision was wrong and the hollering begins, my husband gets a gesture from me . . . except he has the luxury of knowing what that one means without even guessing.

Who else but a farm wife would go back for more the next time her husband needs her help? For the life of me, I can't figure out where those marbles went.

This column by Karen Schwaller first appeared
in the *Sioux City Journal.*

BEAUTY AND THE BEAST

I'm not gonna lie.

It was with great shock and disbelief that I read recently that Gwyneth Paltrow beat me out for the title of "World's Most Beautiful Woman."

I'm not saying it created an avalanche of emotional and self-esteem issues, but it's safe to say that I don't wear black just because I'm such a big Johnny Cash fan.

It did give cause for reflection, though, on what beauty really is.

And the truth is, it depends on a lot of things.

I remembered when our children were small and just venturing out on two and three wheels. I could keep up walking with our daughter as she was riding a tricycle and I pulled her brothers in the red wagon. But once she moved to a bicycle and her brothers put the lead foot down on their own tricycles—even on a gravel road—it became clear that I would have to get myself a bike if I didn't want to eat their dust.

Being a young family with only one of us working at the time, I could not afford to buy myself a new bike. Thus, the lure of garage sales finally broke me down, and I found myself in the garage of a woman who had one for sale. As I was examining it, she said to me, "I think you'll really like it—it has a nice big seat."

At that point, I'd like to have swatted hers.

It may have been the onset of my very first frown line. But the fact remained that I needed my own bike for more than one reason.

If you're a farm wife, you've weighed feed rations, calves, pigs and your options. But weighing ourselves can be scarier than coming face to face with a protective new mother out in the barn yards. And if it isn't bad enough to face the music that disguises itself as a bathroom scale in the corner, then our work sometimes calls us to find ourselves on the scale at the local elevator.

For the farm wife, this whole scale thing not only haunts us on T.V., in magazines and in our bathrooms, but now it comes to the work place. Oh, the injustice of it all.

During planting time in the tractor, I often wonder if—among all of those monitors and push-button boxes with lights—if there isn't some kind of secret satellite screen that tells the weight of the person in the buddy seat; some kind of sacred chip that tells the monitor if the person in the buddy seat has eaten too many of their own chips.

If I've ever ridden with you in your tractor, I don't want to know.

But as we go about life and hear about the "beasts" of beauty pageants, the running for the Most Beautiful Woman in the World, and are bombarded with ads that cause us to painfully compare ourselves to all those flawless, air-brushed women in the magazines and in country music videos, I wonder what real beauty truly is.

And the truth is that all depends on where you live. Because here in farm country, true beauty runs deeper than what we see on the outside of a person.

Farm women may not fall into all the traps of fashion and fads, but in order to contribute to the family business, she can carry feed bags, feed and water buckets and lift hay bales. She can drive a tractor and manage the chores. She can come home from a full day at the office, to start in on her next eight hours of work keeping the home and family going, and working on the farm. She has hands that are strong enough to help load pigs, and soft enough to welcome a new baby into the neighborhood. Her shoulders are strong enough to bear the trials that sometimes come with farm life and weak enough to know when she needs someone to lean on. She has a heart that is generous enough to include all people, yet bruised enough from learning life lessons from farm life, and from people whose motives are less than honest.

She may have lines in her face, but it's from weathering the same storms as her farmer husband. She feels the emotional side of every issue—and on the farm, there are plenty of issues. When those issues affect her family, she feels it the most intensely.

And yet, there she is—a family's glue dressed in denim and dirt, sweaty hair and manure-covered shoes...all the truest accessories of a farm wife and mother. And she stays because she loves this life, and those in her home who make it all happen.

Now that's true beauty. Be proud, my fellow farm ladies.

This column by Karen Schwaller first
appeared in *Farm News*.

IT'S THAT CIRCLE THING

Next to medical people, tax lawyers and friends of Dr. Kevorkian, I can't think of anyone who knows more about life and death than farmers and the farmer's children. Farm kids experience a lot of things—most of which involve layers of grease, animal doo-doo or otherwise unearthed hoards of long-lost hog jowl fossils or sheep tails that eventually show up in the dryer.

But if the truth were known, there are those who are well-rounded in school, some of us who are well-rounded only when we look in the mirror, and others who are more well-rounded when it comes to real life and the lessons it has to offer.

A few years ago my husband was helping out with the chores of our vacation-bound neighbor, who raises quite a large number of feedlot cattle. Naturally, since any day working over there is, by nature, "Bring Your Kids to Work Day," our two (then) eleven-year-old sons lapped up the chance to go and be around that throng of four-legged leather bags, even if it meant getting up at 5:30 a.m. on a Saturday. (Going to work with Mom at the church any day of the week is somehow less gleefully anticipated.)

In these days of computers and video-everything, it still blows my mind that these two would rather walk around in cow dung all day, especially out in the cold. I'm certain that they must have suffered a severe trauma of some kind when they were babies.

When Saturday came, they could hardly wait to spend the day there—and spend it they did. They fed cattle and more cattle; they investigated how some of the machines around there worked; they horsed around and occupied themselves when there were things that only the grown-ups should do. "You'd think they'd be bored out of their gourds," my husband said. "But they seem to have fun."

But the fun wound down to a minimum late that afternoon as they were walking the cattle yards. They came upon a heifer that was having a calf, and having trouble. When the vet arrived, it was confirmed that the calf inside of her was dead. Doing a cesarean section would have been unnecessary expense for a calf that was already dead, and a cow that was also in bad shape. That meant only one thing—put her out of her misery.

My husband hates that job, because the farmer in him is devoted to keeping animals alive. I think he'd rather take a beating himself than have to shoot an animal. Our sons have seen animals die—pigs, sheep, kittens and their dog—that they still miss to this day. But there's something about ending the life of a living being that goes against everything the farmer stands for and believes.

I had happened to call my husband about the time all of that was going on, and one of our sons answered the phone. "Dad's kind of busy because we have to shoot one of the cows," he said with a trembling voice.

Then came a quiet sob.

I held back my own instant tears because I know how hard it can be to watch that happen, even as an adult. Farm kids struggle to understand, too.

"Well," I said as I tried to get the words out as easily as possible. "God gave farmers special hearts, didn't He? They're supposed to take care of God's animals, and sometimes that's the only way they can take care of some problems."

"I know, but I still don't like it," he said, struggling to hold himself together.

The job got done, however, and the cow was taken to the locker. And when they came home late that night, I got to hear about it from our sons as they stood in the porch with their boots and coveralls on, and heads hanging—looking like they'd just lost their best friend.

"I didn't like the noise of the shotgun," one said. ". . . and it was sad when we took her to the locker because we could see where we shot her."

And he couldn't say anymore.

It was a mournful, quiet moment, even with five people in the room, but finally their dad spoke up amid their quiet display of compassion.

"You don't have to feel bad crying about it, guys," he assured them. "It's just one of those things that needs to be done. It never gets any easier, but sometimes you just know it's the only thing you can do to help an animal."

And perhaps they became tried and true caretakers for God's creatures on that day—branded as true farmers. Every farm kid reaches that milestone eventually, but it doesn't come without an emotional price tag.

On the flip side, our ewes had also started lambing about that time. That weekend they got to watch as one ewe gave birth to two very big, healthy lambs. They were excited as they watched their dad pulling them out into the world and helping them get something to eat from their mother.

"That was awesome," one of them said. "It's a lot more fun seeing something be born than it is to help something die."

Truer words were never spoken. The mystery of life and death had come full circle, and they were there through it all.

And as a mother of twins myself, I couldn't believe that mother ewe stood up through her whole birthing process. Of course, an animal that can't even speak up and call me a wimp had no trouble making me look like one.

We all have our crosses to bear.

This column by Karen Schwaller first appeared in *Farm News*.

THE POCKET KNIFE

There are not many things in this life that a farmer can count on. He can't control the climate or the rainfall, the frost or natural disasters. He can't control the markets, the bureaucrats in charge of foreign trade, or whether someone in China will decide his corn isn't good enough for what they're looking to buy.

One thing that a farmer can count on is his trusty pocket knife.

For farmers, a pocket knife is almost god-like, second only to his pair of pliers—the crowned jewel of all pocket-held tools. Yes, if a farmer loses his pliers, it's like losing an appendage, but the pocket knife comes in a close second . . . sort of like Al Gore.

If you think about it, the pocket knife is one of the most valuable tools a farmer has besides his wife or the power-take-off shaft. It's lightweight, comes in many different colors, and they come with many different combinations of tools, all nicely tucked in together. No matter what your frustration, if you have a pocket knife, you can find your way out of it and be home in time for supper.

Pocket knives are multi-functional for many who purchase them, but for the farmer, it takes on a whole new meaning. The farmer uses his pocket knife as a bale breaker when the twines won't just slide off with a firm thrusting of the bale against the knee. He will use it as a scalpel and dissecting tool, a manure scraper, rust remover, a stirring or mixing instrument, a measuring tool, a jimmying tool, a depth finder and seed locator during planting time, a screwdriver, and a passer of time while he waits for a ride by whittling a hunk of wood and thinking about what he's going to do next.

There are times, however, when his pocket knife must take on other uses. Sometimes his wife will forget to put silverware in his lunch, and so the pocket knife becomes a dining utensil unlike any you'd see at the White House, and probably with manners to match. When she prepares a ham sandwich for his lunch and a piece of ham gets stuck between his teeth, it becomes a toothpick when the real kind isn't available. It sometimes serves as a can opener, a cake server, and an apple slicer. It transforms amazingly well into a kitchen tool with a simple scrape of the blade against blue jeans or coveralls to get the chunks off.

I remember the trauma of my husband losing his pocket knife in the barn once. We had just bedded the pigs for the night when he reached for it and realized he didn't have it. Right then and there I realized there is a distinct difference between the way women and men deal with these kinds of crises. I just thought we'd go out and get a different once, since Christmas was coming and it would make a nice gift. He, on the other hand, lamented over it and wanted *that* knife back. Needless to say, all five in our family got on our hands and knees in the straw and began combing through the pig pens in search of his pocket knife.

Would you believe we found it?

Not all that long after that, our son (who was about eleven at the time) asked me, "Mom, have you seen my pocket knife?" I realized then and there that I was in this thing for the long haul.

This column by Karen Schwaller first appeared
in the *Sioux City Journal.*

HISTORY COMES DOWN

I witnessed a little bit of history recently.

Some friends of ours demolished their barn, which was almost a hundred years old, and I'd be lying if I told you it wasn't a sad occasion. It's hard to describe what a barn truly means to the farm family.

The barn is an anchor—a beacon, a place to call "home" for livestock—a protector of their health and well-being; and an enormous symbol that assures us that we are home. It's a sense of pride they have in seeing the barn standing guard over all they are working for—even holding it sacred, as it contains some of the bounty from a growing season for which they gambled all they had for another year. It stands as a testament to the story of agriculture, to that of yesterday, and to those who had the grit to do it "back in the day," when it was a hundred times physically harder to do than it still is today.

I marvel over the craftsmanship of the barn; how long it must have taken men to build them back then, and how many neighbors it brought together to put one up. And once it was put up, those neighbors came together again during threshing season to help each other get their oats and straw in the barns. They were brought together by agriculture, and the farmer's barn.

Homesteading farm families back then most often built the barn before they built the house, living in the barn until the house was finished. Again, a testament to the importance of establishing a living, caring for livestock and putting their needs before the needs of the family. In that spirit, agriculture hasn't changed much in these past years.

The barn is a monument to hard work. It says "rural" and "family" like nothing else I can think of.

And what about the stories that a barn could tell? They are places where important life lessons are taught and learned, and where the seeds for a lifelong love of land and animals are often planted—especially among the youngest of aspiring farmers and ag workers. And it also offers a place to teach a sense of responsibility.

Someone I know told me the story of how, as a teenager, he got home one Saturday night at 4 a.m. Sneaking up the steps so his parents wouldn't hear him, he met his father, who was coming down at that same time. His father was snapping the cuffs of his work shirt, and while never stopping or looking at his son, he said, "Get your clothes changed, Jimmy, it's time to clean out the barn."

And so, without any sleep that night, Jim spent the rest of that night and the whole next day cleaning out the barn with a pitchfork.

He never stayed out that late again.

Once again, the farmer was the teacher, and the barn provided the lesson.

The farmer and his children spend a lot of time in the barn— filling it with livestock, feeding it, bedding it and cleaning it out. The farmer is the first teacher to his children of the lessons in life and death. They gather together in the barn to oversee the births of many a pig, calf, lamb or goat; and sometimes they gather together again to watch some of those same animals die. And they mourn there together.

When crisis or tragedy strikes the farm family, the barn calls them still—because the animals inside need to be cared for, even when the farmer and his family are suffering.

In those times, the barn offers them a place of solace to sort out all the things in life that the family can't understand—and sometimes a place in which to be angry with and bargain with the Almighty, in private.

The farm family works and sweats together there as it vaccinates, sorts and loads animals out of it, nurses animals back to health, and fills the hay mow on what seems like the hottest days of summer.

If the heart of a farmer is to protect his family and those beings under his care, then the barn stands as the protector of the farmstead. It stands the test of time, though perhaps looking weathered over that time. But even then, with a brilliant sunset behind it, it's still a breathtaking silhouette.

The Amish raise them. Southerners dance in them. Rural people admire them. They remind us that the generations before us were here with the same love of the land that we hold today. They have paid it forward and left their mark—with old barns standing as reminders of a simpler time. No wonder barns are so nostalgic, and so historic. You sure don't see new barns going up today.

Farming has changed, but the farmer and his dreams have not.

As I watched our friends' old and weathered barn come down, I couldn't help but think that if the barn could speak, maybe it would say it was relieved, after nearly one hundred years of service; that it'd been a long time, and it was getting tired, and it was time to close that barn door for the last time.

"Well done, my good and faithful servant." *(Matthew 25:21)*

This column by Karen Schwaller first
appeared in *Farm News.*

IT'S TIME FOR THE MARKETS

I don't know how many times I've heard it, but it's been plenty.

There is probably nothing more fulfilling for a farmer than to plan his lunch around the noon news hour so he can keep up on what's current, what the weather is going to do, and of course, the farm news and what the markets are doing.

(Well, maybe that last one isn't always the fulfilling part.)

For many, it's a simple matter of lightly brushing the larger-sized chunks of dung off the shoes, placing a greasy cap over in the corner on the porch, and washing the morning's work off the hands. The rest happens automatically.

But for farmers with smaller children, it can be a bit more of a challenge.

I learned from my own father, who governed over a flock of seven children. With all of the bickering, food comparisons (i.e.: "How come he got more than I did?"); jabbering and all-around deafening kid-mania going on at the table while he was eating and trying to hear the markets, he was reduced to an occasional, "Quiet! I'm trying to hear the markets!"

At that point, a tornado could not have ripped us from our seats, because just like E.F. Hutton, when my father spoke, we listened. Sneezing could have rendered us incapacitated. I'm certain that, being fourth in the birth order, I heard it many times before I was born and shortly afterward. My mother has never told me so, but I'm also certain that my first complete sentence was, "Twiet! I'm twying to hea-o da mawkets!"

How proud my father must have been and what a cunning sense of humor he had. I was maybe twelve or thirteen back in the early 1970s, when I first remember my dad turning the tables on us. As it was, we kids didn't get paid for walking beans, but he would give us some bushels of beans. Those beans, he explained to us this particular year, were ours to sell. But the deal was, that WE had to listen to the markets, and we could sell them anytime we wanted, for whatever price we wanted for them.

He told us he wasn't going to listen to the markets for us, adding that if we wanted to know what the price was, then we needed to find out. If we missed the markets, we missed the markets, plain and simple.

I wish I had thought of that idea. It was a defining moment in noon-time history around the Art and Judy Schroeder farm. From the day we knew the beans were ours, we would listen to the markets like parents waiting for late teenagers to come home. Not a sound could be heard except for the slurping of goulash, the gulping of milk and an occasional forced whisper saying, "Quit touching me!" followed by a slap on the leg.

How heavenly it must have been for my father, to be surrounded by his family and have it quiet enough so he could hear the noon-time radio—which, to a farmer, is almost as sacred as remembering his wife's birthday.

It hadn't been that quiet around the table since someone burned a hole in the new Oliver tractor seat with a cigarette lighter, and no one was fessing up.

We listened and listened through our bites of dinner, and as the markets climbed, so did our enthusiasm for hearing them. We wondered if we should sell them. "Should we sell them today?" we would ask our dad.

"You're the ones who need to decide that," would be his answer as he reveled in the quiet, and in the interest from his children in his chosen vocation.

That year the girls in our family sold our beans for a whopping $10 per bushel. That same year, our mother sold some for four dollars per bushel.

In the years since, my husband and I had children of our own. It was much the same. The dung chunks lightly brushed off the shoes, the greasy cap in the corner of the porch, the greasy-looking hands cupped around the fork, the noisy dinner guests, the radio blaring, and a dad that would, now and then, yell, "Quiet! I'm trying to hear the markets!"

It absolutely gave me the creeps the first time I ever heard him utter those words to our children; the very same words that were shouted to me and my siblings so many times. Out of habit, I immediately sat up, sat still and ate my dinner. The kids had been "shooshed," and because of the haunting of my childhood noon-time dinners, so had I.

One by one as all of us kids left home at graduation time, we all lovingly received a suitcase and clock radio from Mom and Dad. Both were very practical gifts, and although they didn't say it directly to us, the thought of "Get a job, and don't be late for work!" was the statement it made. Of course we, being teenagers, were happy to oblige. Can you blame them for wanting to see the arrival of a quiet dinner again? With each child that left home, that dream became more and more of a reality. Soon, the markets would be heard without interruption.

Will we want the kids back to visit someday with their families? Of course we will. But only after my husband has heard the markets for the day.

It cuts down on the stress that way—especially for those of us who have been "shooshed" at the table many times by a well-meaning farmer—be it our fathers or our husbands.

This column by Karen Schwaller first
appeared in *Farm News*.

THE DOLLAR VALUE OF A MOM

Happy Mother's Day, Moms everywhere. For all you do for your families every day of the year, you've earned the right to take a day and do some guilt-free lollygagging.

If you're a stay-home mom, a day of role reversal may be just the thing you need to refresh the soul and offer a much-needed change of pace. Lord knows I remember thinking that we had so little excitement in our day-to-day obligations in the few years that I was a stay-home mom.

But during that very special time, I heard something that perked me up. According to the "experts," a stay-home mom's salary was pegged at approximately $120,000 per year, based on her services of child care, cooking, dishwashing, laundry, chauffeuring and all the basic maid work done around the house.

It comes out to about $2,300 per week—and that doesn't even take into account the extra wad we should receive for the task of childbirth. That should kick our salaries up to at least a half million per kid, don't you think? At least for those years in which we actually accomplish that task.

Having children, I always thought, would give our lives some dimension. Unfortunately, I've seen more dementia.

The first two or three years after our twins were born, I felt like I spent half of my time wiping floors, fannies and noses, and the other half straightening rugs, pint-sized disagreements and my hair, which on occasion would resemble Roseanne Roseannadanna's in the 1970s.

My husband used to check in during the morning once in a while just to see if I was "swinging from the light fixtures yet."

I was swingin' inside, baby.

In those times—three children aged two and under—a day out alone seemed more unattainable than winning a $50 million lottery ticket.

It's mind-boggling how busy the average mom can be, even with today's modern conveniences that our own mothers never had. I don't know how my mom did it with seven kids. As I look back on it, she made it look somewhat effortless, even though I know there were times when she'd have rather banished us to the grove and tossed table scraps out to us to keep the yelping down.

Surely it can't have been much different than that, just sitting at the family dinner table with all those kids. I can't imagine being the parent of that pack-wolf-like round-up every day.

Patience and exasperation are two trademarks of almost every mother. And they should be—it seems like they go hand in hand. When you run out of one, the other kicks in.

One time our (then) five-year-old daughter asked what it meant to forgive someone. I went to great lengths to explain it so she would understand, and I felt good about the one-sided conversation we were having. When I was finished, she looked at me and said, "Mom, I know how to draw a kite. Wanna see?"

Had she heard a word I'd said? I went to great lengths to explain it.

And for the hurry we're sometimes in for our kids to grow up, we spend a certain amount of time reflecting about things as they reach each milestone—learning to swing by themselves, mastering a bicycle, graduating from high school. We take it all in, and when our job with them at home is finished, we'll enjoy those memories as much as we can. Take the memories of all those crazy Halloweens, for instance.

When our daughter was six, she wanted to be a witch for trick-or-treating, and was trying to mentally put her outfit together. She looked at me, wide-eyed, and said, "Hey, Mom—I could use one of your brooms!"

There better be a big bonus in there somewhere for childbirth.

This column by Karen Schwaller first appeared
in the *Sioux City Journal.*

LIVING THE FARM LIFE

Our three grown children have just left our farm with a baby calf in their truck. They're headed in to town to delight the residents of the local assisted living facility with the wonder that a baby calf is. And the quiet has given me a chance to really think about what it means to live and raise a family on the farm.

For us, there was never any question about it. I have lived on the farm almost my entire life—with the exception of college years and my first few years of being a single working girl. My husband, on the other hand, lived on the farm until he was eight years old before his family moved to town. But he lived on the farm long enough to become hooked. It was always his goal to get back to the farm, and once he did, he never looked back. It was always the place where he wanted to raise his family.

For a farmer, there simply is no other place on earth. There is no other vocation. There is no other purpose for his life than to nurture, feed and care for that which God—and only God—can give him. And that includes his children.

Farmers grow up learning the same things that their children do—and they learn many of those lessons earlier than most kids. One of the most important things that surfaces as they grow livestock is the fact that sometimes animals die on the farm. What tremendous insight comes from seeing an animal die—or one which has already died—and understanding that nothing and no one is meant to be here forever. Once a farm kid understands this lesson with farm animals, it helps them to understand the circle of life, and that the circle of life is the same with people.

They see it on the farm at a young age, before they have to see it at the funeral home. They learn compassion, and they know from early on that death is another part of life.

Farm kids understand what it is to be loyal and a true friend—in part because most farm kids have a dog. Someone who is always happy to see them, help them and run with them. Man's best friend is by their sides as they get older and feel sometimes that their friends have gone in other directions. And when that dog gets old and dies, it's a painful experience—somewhere between the loss of a best friend and a hired man. But it's one that helps them understand unconditional love and true friendship.

Spring is always an exciting time on the farm at the Schwallers', with baby lambs and calves coming in. My husband says he never gets tired of seeing a baby calf born and begin to stand up. Seeing new life come into the world on the farm is always a miracle—if only in the fact that the farmer, who has a long list of other things he should be doing, will sit in the barn for as long as it takes with his children, quietly watching the calf be born, and muse in wonderment about the gift and the miracle that life is—no matter if it's human or animal. That time together for the farmer and his children is invaluable, and is very bonding.

Farmers teach their children the miracle that it is to plant a seed in the earth and in turn, receive a bounty from the land. Farm kids grow up knowing that their family "has" some years, and "doesn't have" other years. They know what it is to work until the crop is planted or harvested, to get that hay baled when the hay is ready, and the time it takes to nurse sick animals back to health. They understand the need to measure time by the sun and calendar, and not by the clock. They grow up with dirt and grease under their fingernails, the earth under their feet, and the sun and rain coming from above—all helping to create that bounty that God blesses them with.

Nothing in life can prepare a child for responsibility like farm life can. Children realize early on that animals are completely dependent upon them. They also know that any job needs to be done when the job needs to be done—and not necessarily when they feel like doing it. Farming doesn't work that way. Life doesn't work that way, either. The lessons in "getting it done" are invaluable.

111

There are easier ways to earn a living, but when the farmer removes his cap and wipes the sweat from his brow following a job well done, it is then that you see the true heart of a farmer. He doesn't do it because it's easy. He does it because it's a calling—to care for the earth and all who inhabit it under his direction.

Farm kids either love the life or hate it. At our farm, the kids have caught it—with all three of our children either farming, or pursuing a career in agriculture. My husband couldn't be more proud that our kids love what he does. The lessons he has worked so hard to teach will now be passed on to the next generation of farm families.

As a farm wife, I could do without having to power wash manure off of jeans before they go into the washing machine, stepping into an obnoxious, odiferous farm truck after our boys have been loading hogs; sweeping lamb's tails out of the basement that young kids smuggle in as farm treasures, or holding on through years when commodity prices are low. But by comparison, farm life has given us a lifetime of memories, and a special place to call home for us, and the next generation of farmers.

For the farmer and his family, there simply is no other place. It's the place where their hearts live; there's no place like home. Even if that home is in the middle of a corn field.

This column by Karen Schwaller first appeared in *Farm News*.

FOR THE LOVE OF HOGS

There are fewer groups of words that can strike more panic into a marriage as the group that goes, "Can you help load hogs in the morning?"

Oh, how I remember those days. Of course, the memories I would like to keep forever begin to fade after a while, but those memories of loading hogs are seriously etched into my mind.

You might know.

A local farmer philosopher was once talking about how hogs love to go the opposite way that they need to be going. In the process he said, "If a hog had a head on both ends, it would go sideways."

If you don't understand that, you simply have not raised hogs.

If it weren't for the fact that hogs contain some of the most delicious meat in the world, I would say it wasn't worth the effort. But because our family is a group of carnivores who loves a good breakfast meal, it's completely worth it to grow that of the swine persuasion. I have to say, however, that if breakfast came in the evening, I would be more inclined to cook it. Hogs get a bum rap, but what would breakfast be without bacon, ham or sausage, or supper without a good pork chop, loin or roast?

One of our local bankers was recently remembering his days of loading hogs while he was growing up. We were exchanging stories of how it usually went—the hogs that got past sorting gates and panels now and then, the yelling (at hogs *and* people) when things weren't going well, the picking up of hogs by their ears in exasperation in order to turn them in the direction they need to go when other methods fail, the tears that sometimes followed by younger kids and sometimes wives when the gate was finally closed behind the last obstinate one. And then the apologies.

Loading hogs can be an emotional experience, indeed.

He said, "Loading hogs brings out emotions you never even knew you had."

It's true. Gentle farmers can turn into their own version of Jerry Seinfeld's "Soup Nazi" when things aren't going well out in the loading chute.

I remember coming home from town once with our children when they were of preschool age. Our daughter had been out watching her dad loading hogs earlier that week, and when we got home, we saw that he was working on that job alone.

It was plain to see that it was not going well. After observing that, our young daughter said, "Piggies are (blankety-blank) boneheads."

After telling her firmly that we don't say those words, I also had a firm chat with her father, telling him the same thing.

Though the world loves to eat pork, it's not hard to see that they are possibly the least appreciated specie in the farm animal kingdom. I would feel sorry for them, but they have created many a cold shoulder in my own marriage over the years, and so I go on loving their product, but not necessarily them. I see the same thing happening in the swine barn at our local county fair from year to year.

Over in the sheep barn on sale day, the young 4-Hers are crying, saying farewell to their sheep after they have led them around the sale ring. Fathers are there comforting them. 4-H is quite a learning experience for the very young, as they often get their first taste of selling something they have raised.

Over in the beef barn, the young kids and teenagers are removing halters from their calves with great sorrow, standing with them and running their hands down the calves' faces for the last few times, and walking away from the livestock truck with quiet tears streaming down their faces. Even the dads are sometimes crying right along with their kids. They all comfort each other after that awful moment of separation has come and gone.

But over in the swine barn, the kids chase their hogs out of the sale ring and up the chute into the waiting truck—yelling things like, "Saah! Come on! Get up there!"—making dang sure they get in that truck, and that the truck gate closes behind them.

They don't necessarily want to see them again—they just want the cash.

Imagine where they learned that.

There are a lot of things that are done for the world's love of hogs.

This column by Karen Schwaller first
appeared in *Farm News*.

THE FARMER'S WASHING MACHINE

L et's face it. There are certain things that only farm families do. And we do them without even thinking.

I'm not talking about the usual clichéd things—like the tried and true "farmer's blow" (What you do when you don't have a tissue or handkerchief handy. You just give it back to Mother Nature in a forced and less than flattering manner. I'm certain that Emily Post would not have approved.)

And I'm sure that only an Iowa farm family would need to stop and buy a twenty-ounce bottle of pop on the way home from work because they need another lamb bottle in the sheep barn during lambing season.

But—the farm family's washing machine is a true wonder. Oh, it's not any different than anyone else's washing machine— it's what's *in* them that could be the basis of a good Alfred Hitchcock movie. Scary things go in, scary things come out . . . kind of like feeding babies.

My most menacing story of opening the washing machine lid was when I peered in to put the next load in, and a very frightened mouse was standing in the drum—probably doing disgusting mouse things in there. I'm not sure which of us was more startled, but you can be assured that it had all the makings of an FBI stand-off for a few minutes. Living in an older farm house makes farm wives capable of handling a mouse trap—even with dead mice dangling from the end of them. I may have passed out, because I can't remember actually putting the mouse trap into the machine, but I did, and the mouse was caught and carried outside.

I may have had to repair to the recliner with an ice pack on my head and a heart monitor on for the rest of the evening following such a traumatic event.

Farm moms have enough clothes to wash, too. There are work clothes for the white collar worker(s) of the family, which must be kept separate from the greasy, dirt-and-manure-covered clothes of the farm laborers. And a show of hands here—how many of you ladies enjoy handling clothes that your guys have been wearing when they are spraying? It's the only other brand of "dirty" that might require a mask and long tongs to get them from the pile to the washer, aside from the clothes that came right from the farrowing house on power washing day . . . or on diaper washing day.

Yeesh.

On occasion, the farm wife will pick up something that is lying on the floor, unsure of whether it needs to be laundered. I have to say that a farm mom may be the only one bold enough to pick up a pair of compression shorts and give them a whiff to decide if they go in the wash pile.

We've probably smelled worse things than that out here.

I have washed a lot of filthy clothes in our machine—even some that have seen the business end of a garden hose before they went in.

Our foreign exchange daughter from Germany saw one of our sons come into the kitchen one day, fresh from the hay field, sweaty and very dirty from head to toe. She looked at him quietly for a couple of minutes, sizing up his degree of filthiness and seeing that he didn't even seem to notice it, then said, "My mother gets mad at my brothers for getting so dirty, but my mother does not know what being dirty really means!"

And recently I was visiting with a friend who was telling someone else how disgusting it is to wash handkerchiefs. She asked incredulously, "You can just throw it away with a tissue . . . why would you want all of that in your washing machine??"

I may be incriminating myself here to the guy who does some of the repair work on our washer, but I told her that our washing machine has washed a sea of used red handkerchiefs, grease- and manure-covered jeans and shirts, lamb's tails, paint sticks, and lots of corn.

She had that same look that I had when I saw the mouse in the washing machine that day . . . so I waited to get the smelling salts until after I caught her on the way down.

Good thing she didn't marry a farmer. It's not for weenies, that's for sure.

This column by Karen Schwaller first
appeared in *Farm News*.

THE MEALS-ON-WHEELS INCIDENT

Farm wives of the world—I beg your forgiveness for making us look so bad. We know our value to the farm family, but sometimes we are so filled with all that life offers us that we rise toward the brim and find ourselves teetering precariously at the edge. Let me explain.

Just recently, I resurrected my once-honed skills of taking lunch out to the field. I hadn't done it since harvest ended, and (truthfully) hadn't missed it all that much. But when it became evident that our pasture fence needed some kind of major overhaul (even by our standards), it became a family project that weekend. The guys gathered up all they needed for the job and headed west.

Our geographical skills pointed to the fact that, since the pasture was out somewhere between Oz and No-Man's Land, they wouldn't be driving into town for lunch, so it became my job to take it out to them.

SO, when the time came I gathered up all that I needed—taco meat, taco shells, cheese, condiments, taco chips, watermelon, cookies . . . you know, the usual American fare . . . and I also headed to the pasture. And ladies, here's where the plan headed south as I headed west.

First of all, I thought I knew where the pasture was—I had been there before, though perhaps under the cloak of darkness. While it's no secret among my family that I cheated at map skills class in the fifth grade (with a nun teaching it, no less), my memory was of no help at this time either. Mid-life is so inefficient.

After a NASA-like phone discussion with my guys, I tripped over the road and landed in the pasture. "Houston, we have splashdown."

I got out and started to prepare the goods . . . or, I would have, if I had brought along any utensils or even silverware to do the job! My mind raced back to field lunches I have packed for my husband and sons over the years, forgetting to include eating utensils. Yogurt can be gulped from the carton or scooped out with the lid—which they have all done; pocket knives come in handy for stabbing peaches or mandarin oranges—though there are probably organisms living in our farmer guys that will baffle scientists for years following a lifetime of boot-scraping and dining with the same knife. Though it sounds as grizzly as can be, a few swipes on their dirty pant legs and a brief sunlight inspection afterwards usually deems it ready for lunch box use if necessary.

Of course, by now our son was headed toward the car ready to eat, so I scrounged around to see if there was something I could use to dip out taco meat and serve up watermelon. How I wished I had brought my husband's pickup truck—I knew I would find something of use to me in there for this task. (But I'll deny it if you ever tell him I said that.) I'm not sure, but I think Bin Laden could have hidden in there for a few months without being noticed.

About that time, my son said, "Hey—I have an idea." He began to guzzle a sports drink, and taking a breath between gulps, he said, "I have to drink it down to there," and pointed at one of the grooves in the bottle. When he had accomplished that mission, he got his pocket knife out and began to cut the top of the bottle off. Once the cap was placed back on the bottle top and turned upside down, we had a meat scooper.

It was a work of art; a real display of American college kid ingenuity. Possibly a new patent idea for the Acme Company. If necessity is the mother of invention, then at least my son could be proud of *that* mother.

"His brain is much younger than mine," I reasoned, thinking that I was really going to have to stop putting off that visit to the wizard to see if I could get a new brain. In all truthfulness, I've always thought that if I remembered to feed the kids, I was having a good day . . . I guess you can't bat a hundred percent every time, especially when you're so busy dropping the ball.

Ladies of the farm—I apologize to you for casting such a dim light on us with my hasty forgetfulness. But if you ever do find yourself in that situation, I wish all of you a kid who can think on the spot like ours can. God always saves the day somehow, doesn't He?

This column by Karen Schwaller first appeared in *Farm News*.

THE NOTORIOUS TREE-TRIMMING INCIDENT

I believe every married couple walks that fine line of insanity when it comes to the issue of long-term home improvements. The only thing is, when they start talking long-term housing, it's soon realized that their marriage may be apparent only for the short term.

It happened to us a handful of years ago when we decided to spend money we didn't have to move a house onto our farm. Seemed that was our first mistake due to the fact that most (if not all) of our conversations about it began at midnight or later, after my husband would return home from his factory job in town.

After we decided to go for it, we had to start making room for the house at its new location on the farm. In this instance, it meant some trees would either have to go or at least be heavily trimmed.

My husband decided he didn't have the heart to cut down the old, huge cottonwood tree standing (kind of) in the way just to make room for our new house, so it was decided that trimming it was the answer.

It was a Sunday afternoon, and deciding we should get started on this tree-trimming project, we naively headed outside with the chainsaw and a vision of the American dream. When a hydraulic line broke on the Farmall Super M in the process of getting the job underway, our American dream took a brief detour. When a chain for the saw was ruined shortly after the trimming began, it was obvious that the thunderheads were beginning to form.

After those crises were resolved came the job of getting up in the tree and doing some major cutting. My husband positioned the extension ladder to its highest position and climbed it, chainsaw in hand, to the limb that he was going to amputate. I was reminded by my husband to get the ladder down before he began sawing.

So, thinking the huge limb would fall somewhat away from the tree, I literally did what he said—took the ladder down. But I placed it on the ground right next to the tree unbeknownst to him. That was the next mistake.

Being a nervous Nellie up there—and holding a running chainsaw—my husband carefully positioned himself in the crook of the tree branches so as not to fall or cut something valuable off of himself, and began sawing. I watched proudly from ground level until the limb fell to the earth, the heavy end landing directly on top of his brand new extension ladder.

At that point, I was wondering if the car had any gas in it.

Breaking the news to him was not easy, because I knew what his reaction would be. It was up to me to get the limb off of the ladder, since it was my frustrated, very angry and very uneasy husband's only way out of the tree. I wasn't sure at that point if it was him or me who was "up a tree without a ladder." After several expletives from above, I got the skid loader and tried unsuccessfully to get the heavy limb off of the ladder.

"Go get the ($%#*$&) tractor!" he demanded of me, as he was feeling more uneasy and more angry as every minute passed . . . not unlike what I was feeling.

I scampered to the machine shed and got into the cab of our aged One-Ninety Allis Chalmers. I'd only driven it a couple of times at that point, and couldn't remember how to start it—especially under such duress.

Nervously sitting there looking at buttons, gauges and knobs, I tried to remember.

Then, I heard him.

"You have to pull out the (#@$%*&) knob!" he shouted from the tree.

"Oh man," I thought to myself. "I hope like hell this thing starts."

I got the tractor over to the tree, lifted the loader bucket all the way up, and he got down without needing casts or crutches afterwards.

Quite visibly angry at my stupidity after he reached grass, he jerked the skid loader around and got the limb off of the ladder. He then examined it with all the speed, dexterity and prowess of an emergency room physician.

"Well, it's not bent too badly," I reasoned, trying and failing miserably at making things seem better than they really were.

"Yeah, but I wonder how much it's weakened now, (expletive-expletive here)," he retorted angrily.

At that point, I was thinking I should have left him up there until he could get over some of his anger. That was even though I understood that his nerves must have been raw at the thought of spending the winter on that tree branch with the companionship of the chainsaw if he couldn't get down.

Quite frankly, that didn't sound all that bad to me either.

You can imagine how the rest of the day went, but I can tell you that the house eventually did get moved and we've been in it for a few years now. I guess he got over it, and I did, too.

Trimming the Christmas tree seems a lot easier on the marriage than trimming a cottonwood. But then it would— Christmas trees are only around for the short term.

This column by Karen Schwaller first
appeared in *Farm News*.

THE FARMER'S AFFECTION

If you're a farmer's wife, then we know that you have fallen in love at least once in your life. We also know that you have spent much of your time since then falling into (and stepping into) things you haven't always seen coming, and some that you have seen coming—cow pies, barbed wire fences, and the occasional friendly reminder from your banker via the mailbox, saying that you need to sell some grain before you get to have a personal relationship with the county sheriff.

Falling in love is easy, but as they say—staying in love really can take some work. The diamond—the crowned jewel of all precious stones—seems to get the official "okie-dokie" as the best way for a man to tell a woman that he loves her. But over time, that diamond can often be out of range for your average farmer—especially in years when shopping for a tractor or manure spreader is necessary; or in those years when paying the bills becomes larger than the list of Elizabeth Taylor's ex-husbands.

If you're a farmer's wife, surely you have noticed there are many . . . well, less expensive ways in which your farmer husband can show you all year long that he loves you. Here are just a few every-day examples:

*When you're out working together in the hog or cattle yards, he offers to take the deeper end, which is much more full of natural fertilizer.

*He doesn't yell as loudly at you when you do something wrong while loading hogs. This is a tricky one, however, and can be directly related to how well the hogs are loading. If it's not going well, the farmer will most likely find himself driving them to the buying station in bachelor style. Temperaments can be as unpredictable as the grain markets, and once that job begins, there's no turning back. When the trailer door is finally closed behind them all and you're wallowing in the aftermath, that's when the vodka is usually needed by all parties involved, no matter that it's only 7:30 a.m. at the time. It could save the marriage on hog loading day.

*When you can't open your twist-off beverage and need his help with it, he will work to find a clean spot on his handkerchief to use in order to help him get the job done.

*He offers to take the role of veterinarian when it becomes apparent that a prolapse needs to be repaired. While you're skilled at sewing things in the house, the farm wife gets the job of handing him the things he needs so he can do the sewing out in the barns. Keep a feed bucket handy, though—your lunch may show up again. Yeesh.

*He cleans up your hair dryer before giving it back to you after using it to keep a new baby lamb warm. You have to save them all, you know. Nothing is spared in that process—including dry hair.

*When the calves get the scoots, he hoses off his own manure-soaked jeans outside before he brings them into the garage for later laundering in the house. Even then, you hope for a nice day because the combination of high temperatures and manure-covered jeans can curl the hair in your nose; and who knows what would happen to the paint on the car in the garage with the source of such noxious fumes so close by?

*When he spits his tobacco out, he becomes a one-man Federal Aviation Administration team and checks the wind speed and direction first, being sure to aim clear of where you are standing. That would be important. Yes. Important.

*He acts just as mad as you when the sheep get out and eat all of your flowers and half of the garden. Secretly, knows he better not say anything about the garden usually looking like CRP acres in previous years, leading the sheep to think it's fair game for grazing any other year. To my husband's dismay, they left the rhubarb this last time.

You might know.

*He cleans out a spot for you to sit in his truck. Let's face it—during the fall harvest, the farmer's truck is filled with all the necessities of life, right down to bathroom supplies, food and beverage needs, tools for any job he may encounter at that time of year, and a wardrobe for hot, cold or rainy days. It all takes room, and if he clears a spot for you to accompany him for lunch on a rainy day in the fall, you know you've made the cut. The farmer must be careful, however, of the size of area he clears out for you to sit. Too large of a spot, and the farmer's wife could leave him to dine on his own.

For a while.

*He apologizes as he tells (or shows) you of a pair of jeans he tore that day, knowing how much you hate to mend blue jeans. It's a little reminiscent of the hog-loading process—complete with the eye rolling, occasional language, and the vodka coming out during and after that whole obnoxious repair process.

So ladies of the farm, take heart. You've already taken his, and if diamonds are out of the question for you this year, look at all the other ways your farmer tells you all year long that he loves you. Even if you don't see it coming.

This column by Karen Schwaller first
appeared in *Farm News*.

SAYING GOODBYE TO CASEY

There were many things during the winter of 2000-2001 that we didn't like—the snow, the snow, and well, all the snow we got. Then there was all the moving of the snow, the melting of the snow and the cost of heating our home, which was directly related to all the snow we got.

As we worked on getting through the winter, the coming of March meant that spring and its promise of new life was not far away. But at our house, it brought with it some news that would prove devastating to our family—our dog was seriously ill.

We got Casey as a puppy during the summer of 1996. Naturally, it didn't take long for our kids or us to become attached to her. She was playful and lived to please everyone around her. She greeted us at every homecoming, and really never caused us gray hairs over all the things that puppies are so well known for. For whatever reason, Casey just never did all the usual puppy stuff.

As she grew and became a part of our family, she eagerly learned the how-to's of chasing livestock and helping out wherever she could. She liked being around people—especially those who would pet her.

When my husband noticed that she wasn't eating and "didn't seem right," he became concerned and took her to the vet, who did his voodoo and gave us things to watch for. A couple of days later after a morning health check found her extremely weak, my husband was pretty certain that her life was in question. He told the kids before school that they may want to go and see Casey because he didn't know if she would be alive when they got home from school. They were stunned, but through brave tears, said their farewells to her before they had to get on the school bus, and we all hoped for the best.

We found ourselves in the vet's office again that day. This time, the news was not encouraging. Tests were done, and it brought the news that we were praying we would not hear—it was certain that Casey was going to die, and soon. A difficult, but necessary decision was made, and Casey quietly slipped out of her pain. Our new red pickup gave Casey her final ride back to our farm—her only home.

We knew our kids would be devastated, and we were right. I met them outside as my husband brought them home from school, and we all cried together over the loss of an animal that meant more to us than any of us really realized. We said good-bye to her as she lay in the back of the pickup, and quietly and methodically, my husband went about the task of burying her on that cold winter day. It hit him especially hard, as he said it was like losing a friend and a hired man.

Through it all, we recalled bittersweet memories of how she was frightened of firecrackers on the Fourth of July, and once raced into our kitchen as I opened the door to go into the house. (I know where farm dogs hang out, and she was not going to win that one.) There were the times when the pigs got out, and she would chase them tirelessly to help get them in. We laughed at how my husband had accidentally discovered her keen intelligence one afternoon as he was working on a project in the machine shed. He pinched his finger on something, and out came a few expletives. When Casey heard the profanity, she immediately took off running toward the pig yards, looking for one to chase in. (Apparently, hearing swear words to her meant that there was work to do with some pigs; could this have been a Pavlovian experience??)

The next week as we were clearing the supper table, I was halfway to the porch door with a plate of scraps for Casey before it dawned on me that she was not with us anymore. When I returned to the kitchen, our son asked me what I was doing, and I said, "Well, I was going to take this stuff out to Casey." He said, "I'll do it!" and quickly took the plate from me and headed out to the porch before the same thing dawned on him. She was a habit that we were going to miss.

The last thing the kids did for Casey was to make a cross out of sticks to place on top of her grave once the snow melted. Somehow it just seemed finished then.

Ironically, our daughter had taken a picture as a 4-H project of one of her brothers hugging Casey. What started out as a fun picture has now become a lasting memorial to her. That photo has earned a place of prominence in our house, just as she earned that same place in our hearts.

If nothing else, we learn now and then that it's hard to say good-bye to our friends, even if those friends have four legs. We quietly went on; but we were never the same.

This column by Karen Schwaller first
appeared in *Farm News*.

A MOO-VING EXPERIENCE

When the sun went down on lambing and calving season this past winter, we had fair luck. We lost a only handful of baby lambs, and our sons ended the season down three calves altogether, along with one cow.

As the post season kicked in, moms and babies got to know each other and the babies took advantage of the free, no-strings-attached buffet before them—as all children do. That is, except for one little calf—the one who lost her mother. She had died from some kind of mystery infection, leaving her heifer calf, "Melba," behind.

Melba is a delightful, happy calf—always glad to see someone, and singing to us in order to entice us to come out and feed her. She always lapped up the milk like nobody's business, and seemed to want company. She had to have been lonely with no mother to care for her. Actually, she had to have been the happiest lonely calf I've ever seen.

Melba would always come running when she saw us with the bottle, or if we called her name, she would first answer, then come running full speed ahead, skidding to a stop before she crashed into the gate in feverish anticipation of feeding time. She would stand around to be petted afterwards, soaking in the attention and giving the love right back. Who says animals don't have personalities?

What a cool little calf.

As the days went by, we continued to feed and care for her. One particular day I went out to feed her and as always, called her name. She always came running. This time she did not. I could see her standing there, just looking at me. So I thought, "Well okay—I guess I'll come out to you then."

I did so, and she lapped up all of the milk and just stood there looking at me.

It appeared to be the same amount of warning time parents get when their child officially becomes—and acts like—a teenager.

Nonetheless, I talked to her, petted her head and left, returning the next day.

I called her name, and once again, there she stood, just looking at me. Once again I decided to bring her daily portion over to her.

This time she licked the bottle a little bit and then just stood there looking at me. I wondered if she was sick, but she didn't appear to be any worse for the wear.

After some examination, our guys decided there must be another mother out there taking care of her, sharing her bounty and letting Melba eat.

I couldn't help but contrast that with what would happen out in the sheep barn if the same scenario were to unfold. Only a very caring and forgiving ewe would take someone else's lamb and feed it out. It's been known to happen, but some of them have to be convinced that it's better to give than to receive . . . no matter what you have to do.

When warm weather called for our sons to check the pasture fences, they deemed them in good shape, and the cows and calves were loaded up.

Arriving at the pasture, they opened the trailer door and the cows and calves made a run for it—much like I do when I've gotten a huge bargain at the store and wonder if the cashier has made a mistake.

They all took off on an exploring mission . . . except for Melba, that is.

Melba stood there looking at her new surroundings, as if she was confused, and maybe a little scared. She didn't have her mother there to help lead her, but she did have the humans there who cared for her very much. Somehow that wasn't enough when all of the others she knew were bounding off to new horizons in a place of endless food and water . . . with their mothers.

Our children were all feeling sorry for her, when off in the distance came a cow running toward the trailer. Our daughter's one and only cow in the herd, who had a calf of her own, was coming back. In her own way, she convinced Melba to return with her, and the two of them ran off into the pasture, a family that they had created of their own choosing.

And they never looked back.

Somewhere in that story is a lesson for us all to learn.

This column by Karen Schwaller first
appeared in *Farm News*.

STOP AND SMELL THE ROSES . . .
IF YOU CAN STAND THE FERTILIZER

Being married to a farmer is unique indeed. Although farm wives are virtually all around us, we share a common bond that neither endless fieldwork nor manure-covered coveralls can break.

The men we stand beside are unique as well, each different— yet all woven from the same tapestry of fabric which our Supreme Creator sprinkled with a love of the land and those who inhabit it—whether they have two legs or four.

Growing up in a family of seven children, my sisters and I were spared the joys of daily outdoor farm life, since my parents were thoughtful enough to space the four boys out (between the girls) far enough that they were always the ones to help Dad outside. On the flip side, they were also the ones who always got the new bikes whenever new bikes showed up on our farm, leading us girls to wonder if learning to cook and care for younger children was really that much less important than cultivating or baling. But then, that's a kid's perspective, I think.

But I've learned a lot about farm life since I became smitten with the man who is now my husband. And what a rude awakening it could have been (farm life, that is, more so than married life—although that can also be shocking on the farm, too) if I were a lesser woman.

It began when I helped him chase some dairy cows out of a yard and into a barn. The yard was deep in manure, so just wallowing through it was no tiptoe through the tulips. After my foot sprang out of my boot—surprising me, I lost my balance and

135

my hands sank into a black hole of gooey, well . . . matter. I hollered across the yard that I'd just taken a bath in the mud.

"I hate to tell you this, dear, but that's not mud," he quipped.

It brought me right back to the days of when I was a very young thing, and was "helping" my dad with the cows one day. The same thing happened, and I fell backwards and was stuck in the manure—unable to get myself up. Dad came to the rescue—helping me up and scraping it all off of my backside.

There have been days since that I've wondered if I have honed those "helping out" skills any further than that. How Dad must have patiently (or not) tolerated it when Mom sent us out to "help" him after we had "helped" her in the house so much. She probably actually got a chance to get the work done then.

Today, I'm occasionally the farm wife who gets to do morning chores because her husband needs to leave early. To understand what a stress this task can be, you have to understand that I was born with no instinctive sense of direction (unlike my husband), and with each passing day I seem to have less and less of a memory.

"The sows get two buckets out of the south feed bin," he began. "The sows east of the farrowing house get two buckets out of the south bin. The gilts in the north pen get two pails out of the south bin. The sows in the farrowing house get four pails out of the east bin—three sows to a pail.

"The baby pigs in the farrowing house get a bowl of pellets out of the bucket that's sitting on the south pen on the west side of the farrowing house. The waterer in the back of the barn needs to be filled, and the sheep in the west yard behind the barn need a bale of hay. Then, walk through the hog house, the nursery and the barn to make sure nothing is mixed up," he tells me, handing me a bag of medicine to put in the waterer for the sick pigs in back of the barn, telling me the amount to give and directions for mixing.

By then, I was the one mixed up.

When I came to, the blinds were still moving on the window of the front door—after he'd closed the door behind him. My head was spinning after that list of directions, rendering my brain one big mass of cranial rhubarb. I wondered if I was in Kansas, or Oz. I would take an aspirin before I even left the house, for the headache I knew would soon follow.

Amid all the things a farm wife must deal with day to day, the most important is knowing that, although her husband has chosen a rather time-consuming and odiferous occupation as a way of earning a living, she knows that he is doing all he can for his family. And while it takes some patience, some off-farm income, some visits to junk yards for farm implements (economy-style farming), and a lot of soap and heavy-duty detergent, it's a way of life that can teach you the importance of stopping to smell the roses—that is, if you can stand the smell of the fertilizer.

This column by Karen Schwaller first appeared
in the *Sioux City Journal.*

THAT WAS CLOSE!

There's a fundamental difference between how women and men react to tasks which involve babies of any kind.

I remember when our first child was born, and when she was only a week old, I had left my husband the odiferous job of changing a soiled diaper. As I listened to this first-time father-daughter experience, I suddenly heard sounds of uneasiness emanating from that room. In fact, they were sounds of, well, knowing that I was going to have a big mess to clean up if something didn't get done, and quickly. Having my hands full of the project I was involved with at the moment, I thought I would help the situation via long-distance yelling, "If you're going to Ralph, move that little red and white dress—she hasn't even worn it yet!"

As it turned out, father and daughter both emerged unscathed from that very traumatic first diaper change. He sat down to regain his strength and color.

To us women, changing those dirty diapers may not be the most fun part of parenting, but it's a necessary job that must be done.

Which is exactly how my husband looked at a situation on our farm a few years ago. We were in the middle of lambing time, and things were going along so smoothly that neither of us thought anything of it when we took the machinery to the field that first day to begin spring tillage.

That day, one particular ewe was acting like ewes do when they are going to lamb. She was sorted off and I was keeping an eye on her so I could get her penned up and get the lamb(s)

138

sucking as quickly as possible. The first lamb was born about noon. The ewe looked too big to be done, and was lying around like she didn't feel very good.

"Poor mama," I said to her as I stroked her head. "I know how you feel. I had twins once myself. I hope yours don't eat as much as mine do, though, or you're going to be getting a second job just to keep up."

Finally at 2:30, I called my husband to see if the ewe should have had her other lamb by then.

"Are you sure there are two in there?" he asked. I assured him that she looked too big to be finished, and that she had the same look in her eyes as I did all those years ago as our twins were being born. I also relayed to him that I had seen no visible signs on the ground or anywhere else that she was finished.

"I would think she'd have had the other one by now," he said via cell phone from the tractor some twenty minutes away from our farm. I was thinking that if there was a shot I could give her or something, I could do that easily enough. "Call me if she hasn't had the lamb by three," my husband instructed.

By 3 p.m. I had made my gazillionth trip to the barn for that day to check on the ewes, and she still had not had her lamb. So I dialed up my husband to give him the news, to which he responded, "Can you get your hand up in there and feel around for the other lamb?"

Upon hearing those words, I twisted my face at the very thought of doing something like that. I couldn't believe what he asked me to do . . . and over the phone, no less.

"You mean you want me to stick my hand in there?" I asked incredulously.

"Well, you don't have to, but I'm twenty minutes away and if there's nothing I can do when I get there, I'll have wasted all that time on the road for nothing, and I need to keep going here. We need to find out what's going on in there."

Oh . . . why did he always have to be right about these things? Reluctantly, and with long silenced and heavy sighs between conversation lines, I agreed to do it . . . not believing that I was hearing myself say that I would do it. I hung up the phone, stunned. I could feel my stomach turning.

I slowly put my boots on yet again, found an obstetric sleeve, soaped it up and took those steps toward the barn. I felt like I was in one of those movies where the person nears the house where the killer is waiting inside, and the barn kept getting closer and closer.

"I can't believe I'm doing this," I repeated to myself "I just know I'm gonna hurl." And yet, I knew it had to be done. I'd seen my husband do it a million times with sheep and sows over the years, so apparently a person doesn't die from doing it.

I reached the barn, opened the door, and found to my complete and utter relief that the lamb was almost entirely born! However, she was still inside the sack, and her back legs weren't completely out yet, so my contribution to her birth was that I pulled her legs out and removed the sack from around her face and body. Oh, the exhilaration that the small task provided me! It was nice to help with even that little part of bringing a healthy lamb into the world.

For the first time, I felt like my husband must have felt as he changed the diaper on our week-old daughter. I sat down to regain my strength and color.

That was *close.*

This column by Karen Schwaller first
appeared in *Farm News.*

THAT'S WHY WE'RE IN 4-H

Aside from opening your front door and seeing a *60 Minutes* camera crew, or finding out that your daughter's boyfriend looks amazingly like Howard Stern, there isn't much that can trigger a panic attack faster than hearing your child utter the words, "Mom, I want to join 4-H."

The closest I ever came to becoming a member was taking group 4-H photos for a local newspaper. I got lost a couple of times heading out to the farm homes that were "way out there" and realized that a 4-H map reading project as a child would have done wonders for my time management skills now. (Cheating at map skills class in the Catholic elementary school was, I found, not a good idea now.)

When our daughter said she was asked about joining a 4-H group, I ignored the time factor it would involve, and decided it would be good for her. "It would probably make us grow a little closer—sharing projects and doing things together," I reasoned.

Right. And Madonna will be moving to the farm sometime next month.

The first thing she did was sign up for about fifteen fair projects. I should have seen Madonna on the horizon right then.

Our first project was to make a pillow case to go over a pre-manufactured pillow form. We were to choose a heavy fabric for the pillow case. Our daughter found lots of other fabrics that she liked better, but they were of lighter weight, so we didn't get them, much to her chagrin. "Part of being in 4-H means learning to follow directions," I explained to her frowned-up, ten-year-old-face. Finally she agreed, until we got to the next meeting to

141

do the club project, and most of the other girls had purchased lightweight fabric to make their pillow cases.

I was less than popular.

Then (on top of that), the entire project was on appliquéing and blanket-stitching, neither of which we knew anything about. Our daughter couldn't decide on fabrics for the applique or a pattern, and since I was on a time schedule that day, we had a muffled conniption fit about that until it was decided what to do. Then (matching the mood and mode for the day), she discovered she didn't enjoy doing stitch work.

Weeks and months passed, and we never got anything done on projects. Oh, I got after her, but was usually met with a scowl or a heavy sigh. And, as many 4-H families will tell you, the usual conversation followed.

Five minutes here, a couple of minutes there, her stitch work speed and stick-to-itiveness would have likened to a cross between a turtle and Andy Rooney. She had that two-speed thing going: slow and stop.

The day before the fair was a frenzy at our house, with sewing and stitch work to finish, photos to mount, green tags to fill out, bars and a pie to bake and a picture to draw. As she worked like crazy to get things done in those final hours her frustration showed. "I know you told me to get my projects done, but I didn't know the fair was coming so soon," she cried softly.

Miraculously she got everything done and got to bed late that night—just as 4-H families have done for generations.

As we wandered around the judging room the next morning, I saw spectacular projects coming in. Yet what amazed me was not necessarily the notion that 4-H kids made all of these things, but that these projects were most likely all done the week of the fair!

I watched as a father consoled his young son who obviously didn't do as well as he had hoped. I knew that was coming for our daughter, too, so I mentally prepared my speech.

When we got to the table where her pillow case would be judged, I said to her quietly, "If you don't do well on this, don't worry. We learned a lot, and that's why we're in 4-H."

Nervously, she sat down in front of the judge, and timidly handed her pillow (with the pillow case on that had caused us so much anguish). They visited back and forth, and as I stood at a distance, I heard the judge tell her, "Sometimes, we just run out of time." Knowing the consolation speech was about to be delivered, she got out of her chair, came to me and grinned.

She had gotten a blue ribbon.

Stunned at that news, we both giggled as we left the building hand-in-hand that day. Then it was a race out to the bean field where her dad and younger brothers were walking beans and waiting to hear how she did. It was a joyous moment for her. After that, the fair was a great source of pride for her.

A few weeks later her leader dialed up our number to inform us that our daughter would be receiving her record book soon, and that she would be over to explain how it was to be done. I'd forgotten about the record book. Panic stuck again . . . it was another thing that had to be explained. Would this parade of new experiences ever end?

As we stayed up filling it out until 11 p.m. the night before it was due (of course), we learned the hard way that all 4-H'ers must learn to be pack rats who write down everything, kind of like ol' Aunt Nellie. But after witnessing the personal growth that occurred with our daughter, we wouldn't trade our 4-H experience for anything.

Not even for a chance to see Madonna clipping teeth and tails in the farrowing house.

This column by Karen Schwaller first
appeared in *Farm News*.

LESSONS FROM THE COWS

Pondering the mysteries of life has been done since the invention of the human being, and will be done long after you and I have been put out to pasture. But as we do this, I think there is a lot we can learn from your average cow. Robert Fulgham began our life advice with his "Everything I Need to Know I Learned in Kindergarten." If cows were able to dictate their version, it might go something like this:

"Come into the world with a bang." If you've ever helped a calf be born, you know what it is to do that job while the mother is standing up—acting like what's going on behind her is all in a day's work. Her calf comes plopping to the ground, shakes his/her head, looks around, and starts the adventure of life. Step into your world, make yourself known to those around you, and leave your mark on the world.

"Stand on your feet as soon as you can, and look around." It's amazing to see animals born. They come into the world much like we do, and are standing on their own four feet within minutes of their birth, wondering at the new world around them. Christopher Columbus was surely no less amazed at what he saw than a newborn calf is. Stand up in this world as soon as you can, carry your share of the load, and always be aware of what's around you. You never know where that cow path is going to lead you.

"Beller until someone gives you what you need." You always know when something's up with the cows. When they're hungry, you know it. When they don't like what's happening, you know it. When weaning time comes, you know it. Remember that the squeaky wheel gets the grease—while tempering that with the notion that sometimes the squeaky wheel gets removed, also.

"Be suspicious of strangers." Watching the cows out in the yard is an interesting and peaceful thing. You can stand there and talk to them (hoping that your neighbor hasn't driven in quietly and brought a video camera to show the white jacket people) and they just stand there, quietly looking at you. Our mothers were right—never talk to strangers. The still waters they lead you beside could be dangerous.

"Chew on things awhile first." With four stomachs, cows have a lot to do just eating. It gives me reason to believe that, since it takes so much time for cows to actually consume and process their food, it should take us some time to consume and process the things that we need to think about, too. Cows savor the eating process; we should never rush through thinking about important things, either.

"Use your tail to swat the annoying things away." When flies and insects annoy the cow, she keeps that tail close by to use as a weapon of sorts, defending herself against those who would cross her line of patience. Though many a farm wife has wished that she had a tail (thinking it would get her more attention from her farmer husband), we need to learn to rid ourselves of those people and things who bring us down. Swat them away somehow and move on.

"Stay with the herd." Cows know it—we should, too. There is strength in numbers. If one gets out, soon the whole herd will be out. They hunker together, always sticking together no matter what. Wouldn't it be a great world if we all carried even this one piece of advice with us?

"Shout loudly if you become separated from your babies." Weaning time; enough said. This goes without saying, but it's true no matter if this happens accidentally, or when your babies move away. Always let your babies know where you are and that you are here for them, and always, always know where they are.

"Adapt to your environment." Cows don't care where they are living as long as they have food, water and shelter. We can all take a lesson from that humble attitude of gratitude. It doesn't matter where you are. Home is wherever (and whatever) you make it.

"Keep your backside to the winds of life." When the world turns colder as fall turns to winter, cows know to stand with their backsides to the wind, and to stand together to stay warm. So when your world turns cold in every other sense, turn your back to it so it doesn't snuff out the flame from your spirit; keep on walking, and stick with those whom you know will be there with you always.

A handful of years ago, our boys' two young calves got out of their pen at home, and wandered into the corn field next to our farm. My husband chased them for a time and ran out of patience. He came to get me to help, and it was obvious to me that once they tasted life outside of a calf pen, they didn't want to go back. I tried a different approach—standing before them both and gently calling them by name, inviting them to follow me. Unbelievably, they did so—and were actually led back into the pen, instead of being chased.

The cows' last piece of advice: **"Always follow the One who leads you."**

This column by Karen Schwaller first appeared in *Farm News*.

THE FIRST GIFT OF CHRISTMAS

Every now and then we are jolted into the reality of knowing what's really important in life. Usually it means there has been a crisis or tragedy of a personal, local, national or world scope. But sometimes it doesn't take that at all.

This past year, it took the giving of the first gift of Christmas.

When the heart is moved with compassion, it's like a locomotive headed down a steep grade. There's no stopping it. And that's where the story began for us.

It was the usual holiday hustle and bustle—trying to get the shopping done early for once, get the cards out, the tree up, the baking done, and prepare the house for company. (We wouldn't want people to see how we really live, so that last one takes a while.)

In a move that I hoped would save us a lot of time and head scratching, I asked our kids what they wanted for Christmas. If you know any of our children, they always say they have the things they need—but we know there are things they would like to have. The search continued until one night when one of our sons approached me quietly, sharing what was at the top of his Christmas list.

He told me quietly that he wanted to sponsor a needy child from the Adopt-A-Child Christmas tree.

If our son had been 10 or more years older, I wouldn't have been surprised at all by this wish, but he was just coming out of his 20th year, so of course I was not at all prepared for something like that.

Standing there in the hallway and looking up at him, I asked if that was really what he wanted, making sure he understood that there would be less for him under the tree on Christmas morning, compared to his brother and sister.

"I know," he said. ". . . but I'd rather help a little kid have a Christmas when they might not have one otherwise."

If you could imagine how small I felt at that moment, compared to the magnitude of what he was saying, and the spirit in which it was being said. And if you never believed in the power and the spirit of Christmas before, you would have walked away from that conversation—as I did—saying to yourself, "I believe."

Only this time you would have really, truly meant it.

A name was taken from the tree, and a young boy became the object of our shopping trip which followed. Our son combed the stores, personally selecting each of the gifts he wanted the boy to receive, helping wrap and I.D. them, and delivering the gifts to the store where Santa Claus would pick them up to deliver them to this child, and to all of the children whose secret identifications were on that tree.

I chose a name off of the tree for our family as well, but as usual, because it was something we've always thought we should do to be grateful for the ways in which God has blessed us over and over, albeit undeservingly. Our son was giving up part of his Christmas in order to do this for someone he didn't even know, but still cared for in this anonymous way.

As per his wishes, nothing was said about this to anyone else in the family, until Christmas morning. When our son opened the last gift of Christmas—a box containing a slip of paper that had the list of the young boy's Christmas wishes—the rest of the family wondered what it was all about. As they listened, they heard the story of what their brother wanted most for Christmas, how it was carried out and a list of the gifts he had selected for that young boy.

It was uncharacteristically quiet in the room for a Christmas morning in those moments, and as they listened to the story, they saw their brother in a new light, and their own hearts were overflowing with compassion. They decided they wanted to do something like that next year also. It was a prideful time.

That locomotive was full-steam ahead.

It's amazing how one person's thinking and actions can affect the way other people think. It's a powerful thing, and if used for good, it can change the world, if only one person at a time. Our son has always known it, but this year especially, he and our whole family rediscovered just how much better it feels to give than to receive. It truly was, for all of us, the first—and most lasting—gift of Christmas.

"And a child shall lead them." (Isaiah 11:6)

This column by Karen Schwaller first
appeared in *Farm News*.

THE SIGHTS AND SMELLS OF
FARM PICKUP TRUCKS

There are some things in this life which never go away . . .
zucchini in the garden, vacuum cleaner sales people, bills,
and this farm wife's belief that if you could make chicken
or fish taste like pork or beef, her husband's nose wouldn't turn
up at the thought of eating something that didn't stand on four
legs before it reached his plate.

Yes, some things are sure to be the same forever—much like
the farmer's pickup truck.

Have you ever looked inside one of those things? The pickup
on our farm is an advertisement-on-wheels for Service Master—
albeit, more at some times of the year than others. It resembles
the aftermath of a natural disaster most of the time, and is in
desperate need of some quality time with a gas mask, spray can
and the shop vac.

Oh sure, it looks okay from a distance, but a view from the
fifty-yard-line shows that no matter how hard some mothers try,
some kids just don't catch on to that tidying-up thing.

But it wasn't always that way. How shiny it was at first. And it
was a real novelty—power windows, bucket seats, four-wheel-
drive, and it may or may not have met the criteria that one of our
friends has that a pickup "should look mean."

The best part of it for me was that it once smelled new, even
for a used truck. I was used to his quite odiferous and swine-
infested red Ford F-150, which he cleaned up spotlessly for our
first date. I'm certain that was the last time that pickup ever saw
clean water . . . or even a willing passenger.

The downfall must have taken root a couple of months after he bought his new pickup, in which I put the first scratch. As someone who can operate a semi, my husband successfully uses mirrors in every aspect of driving. Curiously, I waited until he got his new pickup to start practicing using the rear view mirrors while backing up. That came to a halt forever when I scraped up against a barrel situated near the open gate through which I was trying to navigate.

For all practical purposes, I could have captained the Exxon Valdez—and done just as good of a job.

Since that little escapade a few years ago, it's been a pretty steady decline for the pickup. The back window was broken out once, giving us slivers in some pretty interesting places for a long time. One of the doors was bashed in after coming into contact with a snow bank with an attitude. The carpet was removed because of a recurrent heater core problem; the defrost works whenever it feels like it, a hole shows plainly where the glove box once was—while the glove box itself gathers greasy dust in the machine shed. The window on the passenger side needs a dose of Viagra so it will go up at the command of the power switch on the driver's side.

Where we once could put the truck into four wheel drive from inside the cab, we now have to get out and do this flip thing on the rims in order to do it.

And the smell . . . let's just say that when you're taking the pickup to town to run errands, business people can tell that you live on a farm, and they don't even have to ask.

Our truck has hauled live and dead hogs, live and dead sheep, livestock feeders, wagons filled with grain, assorted farm implements, fuel tanks, seed bags, insecticide and herbicide, and it even hauled a new dishwasher home—which my husband bought for us after he even got tired of looking at piles of dirty dishes to wash, with not much time to do it.

A look in the truck today may show you several tool boxes earmarked for specific farm-related projects; some boots, various tools, log chains and a chain binder, boards and nails of differing lengths, tires, the highly-valued stock prod, some fuel- and manure-speckled coveralls which should have been laundered two springs ago; a roll of wire, spray application manuals, aluminum cans, winter clothes (even in the summer); hog manure, and there's occasionally some grass growing in the back.

Things grow well where there's lots of natural fertilizer left behind.

The truck-width toolbox stores even more treasures that a farmer can't be without when he's working—up to (and including) that sometimes necessary roll of toilet tissue for whomever may find it necessary while working away from home. And if you find that amusing, believe me, it beats a cornfield biffy without an accompanying roll of saving grace, even if it comes wrapped in a dusty bread sack.

Farmers have a certain loyalty to their trucks, and perhaps they should. Pickups are there at the start of spring planting and bring exhausted farmers to their homes late at night when the last rows of corn have been harvested.

They're parked at the local financial institution while farmers discuss critical decisions with bankers. Pickups take farmers to keep watchful eyes on their crops, are at the scene of any crop disaster, and are often brought with empathy and helping hands to a neighbor's farm, should a natural disaster strike. They're found lined up for a quarter of a mile in any direction at farm auctions, and take many a farm family to livestock buying stations and grain elevators in the constant hope that low commodity prices won't force them to give up all they're worked for in exchange for a job in town tomorrow.

Bur for all the reasons farmers have pickup trucks, perhaps the most important reason is that they also carry in them the future—young children eager to help, and wanting to be stewards of the land and of livestock; wanting to grow up to be just like dad.

So much can be learned from farmers who spend precious time teaching tomorrow's grain and livestock producers, and it often begins with time spent together inside the cabs of tractors—and pickup trucks.

This column by Karen Schwaller first appeared
in the *Sioux City Journal*.

THINGS YOU SHOULD NEVER BELIEVE

This past Thanksgiving Day, as I listened to my food digest and rubbed my full stomach much in the same manner as I did when there was a miniature human being inside of it, I had plenty of time to think about life and what it was that made me the person I am today.

After much meditation and a handful of antacids, I decided that in the beginning of a life shared with a farmer, it's all the believing you do together which makes it work—that dream of the future, that undying devotion you think you have for each other that time spent together will never alter, and that you'll always speak to each other the way you did in those early years of your relationship.

What a ridiculous folly.

Perhaps many women get fooled by their husbands now and then—it's just that for the farmer and his wife, there are simply more opportunities for it to happen.

It's for that reason that I've devised a lot of things the farm wife should never believe when her husband utters the words to her.

*(Regarding helping outside): **"It'll only take five minutes."** Do you think he's going to have you put on insulated coveralls, boots, a hat and gloves to come outside and help for only five minutes? A farm wife should come outside ready to cut an inch off the end of his nose right away for that one.

*"You won't get full of manure."** (or single words which otherwise mean the same thing as manure.) I have yet to come in from helping outside when I haven't had to wash the end products from a pig's daily diet off of my boots. I made the mistake of believing that line once. My socks were never the same afterwards.

*"Can you find the 7/16 end wrench? It should be right on the end of the work bench."** For any of you who may not have ever had the misfortune of entering our machine shed, you should know that you have to search for the work bench first before you can find anything on the end of it. This is especially true if you need the wrench before his once-a-year shed cleaning, which he has you help with even though you don't know from memory where anything goes—mostly because you've never seen anything in its proper place.

*"I'll probably be home for dinner."** That dinner thing has agonized farm couples for generations. She knows he usually takes a while to come in once he's called, so she calls him in early while she finishes up the meal, then he decides to come in right away—and sees that dinner isn't ready. Next time, she remembers that he came in right away, so she waits until dinner is ready; then he comes in half an hour later because he remembered that dinner wasn't ready the last time she called him in, and he had to wait anyway. When she hears this phrase, she knows she better see the dust behind his pickup coming down the road before she tosses the meat on the grill.

*"You mean that hog check is "gone already?"** This is a good one. Often leaving her feeling like she's squandered the money somehow, she knows that the money went to pay the elevator bill, the feed store, the vet bill or the psychiatrist if they've been married long enough—and not necessarily in that order. Some years, however, most of a hog check could've gone to pay our cable TV bill, which farm couples never get a chance to utilize anyway with all they have to get done.

*"It's not that hard—just try it." These words were once spoken to me—a person who has difficulty using rear view mirrors for anything other than adjusting make-up and watching the patrolman approach my car. I usually turn and look behind me when I back up because that way, even when I'm driving backwards, I'm still going forward. The last time my husband spoke these words to me, I scratched his new pickup. Perhaps we both learned a lesson.

*"Those coveralls look nice on you, dear." Have you even seen a pair of baggy coveralls that enhance a figure? He must really need the help outside.

*"Maybe we can do some work on the house when hogs get to \$50." Farm wives must be cautious of this statement. When he refers to "the house," she must investigate as to whether he means the hog house, the farrowing house or the people house. At times they all seem to be one in the same.

And finally, ***"Have you seen any clean jeans around here?"** While this one might hint at the piles of laundry taking over the basement, the farm wife knows it may also be a hint about the mending pile that has become just as big as the laundry pile. A day of washing will take care of the one problem, and a few Vodka-Sevens will help her through the other frustration of mending one pair of blue jeans at a time, knowing they will most likely be back on the mending pile soon.

We farm wives may not always be geniuses, but we get smarter with every passing year. How I would hate to start over. And I really believe that.

This column by Karen Schwaller first
appeared in *Farm News*.

SELLING THE CALVES

For what it's worth, I think there are few better organizations to be involved in than a local 4-H club.

One particular year brought us a brand new 4-H experience when our kids were in middle school.

It began one summer when our neighbor suffered a major heart attack, requiring a multiple-bypass surgical procedure. He has a large feedlot cattle operation and was now unable to care for his herd. So he called on my husband to care for them in his hour of need. He was also unable to fill his silos that summer, so my husband and our sons did the job with the help of another neighbor. For the first time in his 68 years, our neighbor watched as his work was being done, and was the most difficult thing for him. However, it was the most proud thing our boys felt they had ever done, and they loved the work.

After a couple of months, our neighbor was able to care for his cattle again, and one day he pulled into our yard with a stock trailer behind his pickup. When we approached the trailer, there stood a calf, which he had come to give our boys in return for all their time and work for helping him when he needed it.

"Here's the keys," he said as he handed them a halter.

Our boys' eyes grew wide with surprise and excitement. They had never had their very own calf before, and certainly never expected to get one. Their grins almost didn't fit their faces.

To make a long story short, one calf grew into three by the time all three kids decided they wanted to show a calf at the fair.

The calves were fed and cared for by the kids, and as fair time approached, their work with them became much more time consuming. Breaking them to lead, washing and combing them, getting the calves to trust them, learning their personalities, there was so much to do with them. They were so excited to take them to the fair. They did a great job of showing them, and they had a lot of fun doing it.

Sale day came all too soon. They got up, went to the fairgrounds and approached the beef barn, where their calves awaited their arrival, and the kids all knew what was ahead of them that morning. They washed their calves, taking special care that last time. The halters were put on through moist eyes and with heavy hearts, and the farewells began.

The sale ring was set up in the show arena, where waiting buyers mingled and compared notes. The show arena was fairly quiet. I was sitting in the stands, hoping the kids would do well at the sale, and hoping they would find the courage to walk into the show ring with pride, and that I would hold it together for their sake.

Too soon for our kids, the auctioneer's rhythmic calling began, and the auction began. Other calves and 4-H kids entered the show ring. Some went methodically in and out of the ring. Other kids were having difficulties. Their tears glistened in the early morning sun as they led their calves around. Some hid behind their calves, and others cried public tears with pride in the work they had done for the past year. It wasn't long before it was our kids' turn to enter the sale ring. They gathered up the courage to go out there, and I wondered if they heard the auctioneer, or if they were caught up in the sorrow of the moment. Buyers' heads nodded in competitive bidding as the kids led their calves around the sale ring, and when they finally heard "Sold!" the calves then belonged to a livestock buyer, and it was time to put them on the truck.

Farm kids have known since elementary school what happens to the animals after they're on the truck, and they understand and accept that it's just part of raising livestock. But no matter if you're the 4-H youth or the dad, they're just difficult to sell when you have become friends with those animals.

There were fathers with arms around their kids that morning consoling them, and sometimes, consoling each other. I wiped away tears of my own as I sat in the stands, trying to get those moments on film.

Halters sorrowfully came off, and good-byes were said between man and beast, and our kids were alone together, holding their halters but not their tears. A senior-level 4-H youth approached our kids at that point, and empathized with them, telling them he understood how hard it was to sell calves that first time. This, we thought, was quite a tribute to his character, and to the binds of friendship that are created through 4-H. It spoke of friendship that has no boundaries on age, or limits on whether or not it's cool to associate with someone younger, and to encourage them as an older, more experienced 4-H youth. That is part of what 4-H is all about.

Soon it was all over, and what the kids learned about friendship, showmanship, sportsmanship and citizenship for future years was beyond comparison. There is so much to be learned through 4-H, and even though it creates pandemonium in schedules now and then, I believe it's one of the finest organizations that are available for kids and families.

Even if it hurts sometimes.

This column by Karen Schwaller first
appeared in *Farm News.*

THINKING LIKE A FARMER

Let's face it. It's no news flash that farmers are often known to be great innovators. It's also no big news that, over the years, they have learned that skill out of necessity. It is, after all, the mother of invention.

Most of us have experienced that prices are not always good on the farm, and those expenses just keep coming, and those repairs all still need to be made. When the farmer takes a gander at his check book and sees that buying new just isn't going to happen, he's left to daydream about what it will take to replace the new with the rebuilt or redesigned. It doesn't always look like it came right out of the factory, but most of the time it gets the job done, and with very little cost. Enough of this kind of thinking could render him enough cash flow to farm yet another year.

My husband, who has stayed as busy rebuilding tractor and implement parts as Michael Jackson's plastic surgeons, is always on the lookout for a bargain. Thirty years of farming has taught him that you might "have" this year, and you may not "have" again the next year. It didn't take me long to figure out that my husband could have survived the Great Depression—with the drive he has to make do with what he has, to do things himself, and by being smart about doing necessary things as cheaply as he can.

I hope that last characteristic didn't govern how he selected his wife.

Here at the Schwallers', it's no different when that same farmer undertakes a task in the house. Take, for example, my husband's approach to child care when one of our (then) elementary-school-aged sons was sick and stayed home from school. I had some things going on at work that I needed to be there for, but could have rescheduled. My husband, on the other hand, said it would be ridiculous for me to stay home when he would be home and working outside all day anyway, and could check in on our son from time to time.

Concerned that he still would not be in the house when our son's past 24-hour diet would be seen visibly, (I didn't want to be called home to steam clean the carpet), I said I would just stay home. He, being the farmer and the one used to coming up with his own ideas and inventions, had an idea, of course.

He went to the office and cut a long piece of yarn and grabbed a sheet of red construction paper. He tied the yarn into a hole he'd made at the top of the piece of paper and draped the paper and string over the curtain rod, letting the paper fall to the floor. He then proceeded to explain to me that his plan would work great. Our son would be on the couch (which was next to the living room window—which faced out into the farm yard). If he felt like he was getting sick and needed help, he could pull on the long string of yarn, pulling the sheet of construction paper into full view in the window, and my husband would then, (even if he was outside) see that he needed his help right away.

And there we had it—a father's health care plan hanging from a piece of yarn in the window. And the plan did work perfectly. Fathers of invention get very little credit compared to their gender opposite.

Of course, one of those things that many a farm wife has learned to do, is cut the family's hair. When the hog market first took a dive in 1993, paying for haircuts was something that was slashed from the budget. I had to learn how to do it or let everyone walk around looking like they belonged to the Rolling Stones. It would be years before our children *wanted* to look that way.

After a lot of years of using the apron that separates man from his own severed hair, the string used to tie it around the neck finally wore through and broke. Wondering how I was going to fix this, my husband—who happened to be in the basement barber chair at that time—had an idea right away. Out came the veterinary supplies tub, and he fished out a clean prolapse needle and some string, also used to fix said prolapses. He threaded the needle, then proceeded to sew the string very carefully in and out around the top of the apron, leaving two long pieces at each end so that I could tie it again.

Who knew that livestock female problems could actually contribute positively to household repairs??

It's been said that, to be successful at raising livestock, you have to learn to think like the livestock. While happy that I never did learn how to think like a hog, I do think I'd better first master learning to think like a farmer.

It could keep me in the farm wife business for yet another year.

This column by Karen Schwaller first
appeared in *Farm News*.

THE FARMER'S PICKUP—
GENERATION TWO

If you're any kind of Johnny Cash fan, you know all about it. One of his songs tells the story of how he brought a car home from the auto factory "one piece at a time." While that's not the case at our house, the end of that song really is true.

I remember it clearly. Our boys' driver's licenses came a few years after they started driving. (You know how it is on the farm.) Just about the time they became legal to drive, they had a chance to purchase a well-used 1989 Ford Ranger from a friend.

Here at home that evening I was gathering up the necessary cuisine items needed to take supper out to the field when one of them called me up and said, "Can you bring my wallet when you come? . . . and leave all the money in it."

It was an outright order.

He told me they were going to buy a pickup. (For a piddly few hundred bucks between the two, I thought? Good Lord.)

When I first saw them get in and out of it, they reminded me of those circus bears that ride the tricycles. They're bigger guys, and it just looked funny.

A few years later now, they still look funny getting in and out of it, and they have put hundreds of working miles on it. She's a beaut, that's for sure—with rust eating its way around it, and the machine shed-generated custom paint detailing by the door handles that say, "The Boys." It was put there by a couple of Schwaller boys who couldn't find anything better to do one stinkin' hot summer evening after the baling was done.

They even found a way to upscale without spending any money. They came across a metal logo sign from a discarded Ranch King lawn mower one day. And anyone who has had twins—or maybe just boys in general—can tell you that old adage of, ". . . what one doesn't think of, the other one does." They took that Ranch King piece, cut it in half, switched the words around and screwed them onto the truck near the place where it says "Ranger XLT." Now it says "King Ranch" behind it.

They have now discovered what rubbernecking is, as people wonder if Ford really made a King Ranch Ranger.

Good Lord.

I have to say those two have done a lot of hard work with that truck by their sides. Today it sports all kinds of things often found in a farmer's truck—fencing supplies, corn cobs, clothing for any kind of weather, wrenches, screwdrivers for checking the electric fence without having to actually step out of the truck, binoculars for checking their cows in large pastures, curry combs, syringes, pliers, ropes, tires (even one behind the seat) and chunks made up of various forms of farm dirt and barnyard boot remnants. They even have a lariat hanging from the back window.

And the smell. It's the vehicle they take back and forth when loading hogs, so you know it's slightly odiferous. It was especially so after they hauled one of their baby calves to town last winter in the cab, so they could show their grandparents. The speakers in the truck were never the same after being met with a frightened baby calf's colorectal reaction to being separated from his mama.

I offered to wash the truck once and was met with all the reasons a farm truck should not be washed. Mostly it was because it just wouldn't look cool all cleaned up.

It has muffler issues, so we can always hear when they are home with it.

The rear bumper lets the world know it belongs to a Schwaller kid, with a worn-out FFA-sponsored sticker that says, "I farm. You eat." Logos for both John Deere and Case-IH grace the back window—for the peace-making farmer who chooses to remain impartial.

Now that the Christmas season has arrived, they've found a way to extend their holiday greetings to those they meet on the road. They unearthed a wreath, wired it to the grill, and put Christmas lights on it. But still not satisfied with the manliness of how it looked, they decided that the finishing touch would be a couple of horns from a cow that they had de-horned not long before that.

Now they have a lighted Christmas wreath on the front of their truck with cow horns sticking out of it. Clearly—a man's-man holiday greeting.

Good Lord.

They are truly the "Men in Black," just as Johnny Cash was—only theirs is a black truck instead of black clothing. Well, it's mostly road-dirt-colored, with a little black showing here and there on the cab.

Johnny Cash was right. You'll know it's them when they come through your town . . . 'cause they'll have the only one there is around.

This column by Karen Schwaller first
appeared in *Farm News*.

WHAT THE FARM WIFE KNOWS

For those of you who may not know me, be advised that I tend to have a few irons in the fire most of the time.

From the day I married a farmer until now, I've continued to struggle with knowing which end is up. (At least by the time we got around to having babies, I figured out which end got wet and which one needed to be fed—that has to account for something.)

During a substitute teacher's aide stint at our children's elementary school once, I ran across a piece on real teachers and what they're like. I was rather taken in by the piece and I thought I could come up with a few facts about real farm wives and what they know.

There's a lot to it, so I'll just get to the meat of the thing—which actually is one of the first things about a real farm wife—she can't cook a meal without meat. A farmer will find a way to work meat into any meal.

A real farm wife also knows that:

*. . . her husband keeps time by the calendar—when the crops should be planted/harvested, when the spraying should be done, when the lambing or calving will begin. Since that schedule affects everyone in the house, she knows that clocks are for her urban friends and family, and that quitting time is when the work is finished—and not before.

*. . . even if there were forty-eight hours in a day, there still wouldn't be enough time to get everything done in time to catch *Letterman.*

*. . . "Murphy's Law" comes into play when livestock decide it's time to break out—the later you are getting ready for an event, the more they all want to see in person if your shoes match your outfit.

*. . . she needs to know exactly what her husband wants of her before she commits to anything he asks her. For example: her husband asks her about "going out" on a Saturday night, but it turns out he means going out to the farrowing house or to the barn to check on gestating livestock while he's gone, instead of hinting at something of a more romantic nature.

*. . . even though Sundays are meant for families to spend time together, more farm work can be done on Sunday than any other day of the week because it's the only day the farmer is home from his job in town.

*. . . the sound of the dishwasher running is like sweet music when she comes in from outside after a long day.

*. . . some things do grow legs and walk away—like whips and right-handed work gloves.

*. . . she's often needed to drop what she's doing on a moment's notice to help outside, even though the reverse is not usually realized.

*. . . she has cleaned enough dirt and mud out of her house to claim ownership to at least an acre of land . . . and that mud returns like a stubborn fungus.

*. . . mending jeans and overalls goes along with the job. It's kind of like a hangover effect, because it can be a real headache.

*. . . loading hogs without a stock prod is like trying to sew while wearing oven mitts.

*. . . because of his chosen vocation, animal husbandry most often comes before people husbandry.

*. . . tractors and other equipment will break down when commodity prices are low, and that the parts man behind the counter will most likely ask her something she doesn't know.

*. . . a family who works together can really pile up the manure-covered laundry . . . and that laundry soap, like a nighttime facial mask, can only work so many miracles.

*. . . the timely disposal of newspapers and farm magazines is important if she wants to keep enough room in her house for her family to live without adding on a wing for the storage of those items.

*. . . although she knows it could likely happen, she never wants to hear the words "farm accident" used together in reference to someone in her family.

*. . . her husband can remember the exact date and time of a day five years ago when it rained half an inch, but he has a tough time remembering which day is her birthday.

*. . . her children learn firsthand and at a young age why some years they can have the "extras," and why some years they can't.

*. . . any (non-working) time they have to spend together as a family must count, since today's young farmers have to believe in the quality of time, if not the quantity.

*. . . finally, a real farm wife is content to know her true value, because in many cases it would take the help of many people to step into her solo and varied role as a combination hired man, support person, gopher, transporter of equipment and

food, sounding board, maid, family caretaker, wage earner, bookkeeper, psychologist, and friend.

She might make it look easy, but that's just another of her many talents.

This column by Karen Schwaller
first appeared in *Farm News*.

WHY THE FARMER FARMS

Recently we received a phone call from a panicked farm wife just up the road. Her husband had been seriously injured while working on the farm and she needed someone to call for help and be with her as she fearfully watched it all unfold before her.

Our family arrived about the same time as the local rescue unit, followed by the quickly-arriving ambulance. Rescue personnel hovered over him, and our friend was swooped away in the ambulance. He was then air-lifted out. We watched the helicopter take off from the hospital and fly away until we couldn't see it anymore, our hearts heavy in the darkness of that late night, hoping and praying for the best for our good friend and neighbor. We had done what we could do for him, and for them. The rest wasn't up to us.

It got me to thinking about why farmers do what they do— and for so long.

And the truth is, I don't know if anyone knows the answer to that question.

There are a lot of occupations that are all-consuming. But farmers take that to a whole new level. Often times it's out of necessity. After all, unless they have your same last name, it's difficult to find people that want to work on the farm. And having the same last name doesn't always guarantee the help. There is a lot to do—especially for livestock farmers—and not a lot of help is readily available.

They work against all odds—weather, markets, government regulations, finances, fatigue, frustration and dangerous machinery and situations. And sometimes those things come down on the farmer all at once. There are probably people who need more coping skills than farmers, but at the moment, I don't know who it would be.

We recalled this neighbor of ours who, many years ago when cattle prices were very low, approached his banker to secure a loan to get more cattle. After a lengthy discussion between the two, the cattle trucks made their way to his yard and the four-legged cargo was unloaded. Asked why he wanted more cows when the cattle market blood bath raged on, he said, "Because it's what I know how to do."

Simply put, that's just the way it is with farmers. They don't do it for the money. They don't do it because it's easy. They don't even do it because it's great for marriages.

My father, who worked as hard as anyone I know, was committed to this life. My mother, a city girl who said she never really adjusted to life on the farm in the 50-plus years she lived on one, once heard the farm described as "the farmer's mistress." I know there are many who feel that way, and it's not because the farmer husband doesn't care. It's because he loves what he does with the kind of honesty, loyalty, work ethic and passion needed by anyone who is driven to be good at what they do. And it takes all of him to get that job done—especially when farm help is scarce, and the work is piled up.

He loves it, he hates it. He's too busy for his own good. He has to learn to do everything himself in order to afford it. He has to learn to fix machinery so it will last another year. He has to be on top of animal health issues. He has to know his cost of production and be a good business thinker. He has to run long days on little sleep. He has to know and teach safety around machinery and livestock. An unprotected and running power take-off shaft—or an angry sow or a protective cow who has just given birth—can wreak massive havoc on a farmer's body in short order. He must be determined to never give up no matter what kind of bad things happen. He must always be on top of his game.

And yet he dreams for his children to love this lifestyle as well. With all of the good and bad that comes with choosing life on the farm, he takes it in stride and mixes them both together gently. Most importantly, he not only tells his children, but shows them with his own example and sweat equity that without agriculture, our world has nothing.

As we watched our 75-year-old neighbor being air-lifted away, we talked about the fact that he had been doing the work he loved doing all of his life. And whether or not we understand why farmers choose this life, we know for certain that they would rather have their hands in the soil until their last breath, than spend time in a rocking chair.

It's in their hearts and in their blood. It's their will and their purpose in this life.

And that's why the farmer farms... until the last gate has been closed behind him.

> *"My grandfather used to say that once in your life you will need a doctor, lawyer, policeman or a preacher. But everyday, three times a day, you need a farmer."*

(Brenda Schoepp)

This column by Karen Schwaller first
appeared in *Farm News.*

THE SKY'S THE LIMIT

I t's something I've thought of before, but it really struck me when one of our children took notice of it as we were watching a movie recently.

During the movie, a New York lawyer was coming home from work on city transportation, and as they were coming to a stop, a business caught his eye when he looked up and out the window. He got off of the train there and took care of some business before going home for the night.

It was something I didn't think anything of as we were watching, but one of our children saw that brief scene and immediately commented, "Isn't that something? For some people, that's all they ever see."

I knew exactly what he was talking about. The sky was nowhere to be seen. Most of the time when we look up and out of our windows as we drive home from work, the sky is there to greet us, whether it's light or dark outside.

Being part of the rural population means seeing the sky every day and every night. We don't think anything of it, and probably even take it for granted. That is, until we can't see it....or until we see that it's bringing us bad news. Or that it's not bringing us what we need for our crops to grow. Our sky and what it does is mighty important to us as farm families.

About a dozen years ago our daughter and I were in Chicago, and as we did that tourist thing so well—appearing seemingly less Clampett-like than if we were in, say, New York City—we noticed that the buildings downtown were so tall that there was only an alleyway of sky visible above us.

After I was done being mesmerized by the sheer height of all that concrete, I remembered wondering how people lived like that.

I've wondered since then if there are people who have never seen the horizon, or who have never seen more than an alleyway of stars above them at a time. Or if they've ever had the chance to lay in the grass and watch the clouds roll by above them, and try to make shapes and stories about the clouds as they go by. Or if they've ever sat in their garages and literally watched a pelting storm pass by. Or if they ever get a chance to see the breathtaking colors of a sunrise or a sunset, which only God could create. Or if they've ever seen how stunning a corn field, running combine or a barn looks, silhouetted before a setting autumn sun.

All of this reminds me of a story I once read about a father who brought his son out to the farm in order to show him how the poor people lived. The (truly) poor farmer and his family greeted them and they spent a day and an evening together. When they returned from their trip, the father—feeling as if he'd made his point—asked his son what he learned while staying with the poor farmer. He was stunned at his son's answer.

The son said that, while they had one dog at home, the farmer had four dogs to love him. He added, "We have a pool that reaches to the middle of the garden, and they have a creek that has no end. We have expensive lamps in our house, and they have all the stars in the sky. Our patio reaches out to the front yard, and they have all that land and the whole horizon."

Then came the kicker, as the son's interpretation of the day was much different than that of his father's.

When the boy was finished and the father was speechless, he added, "Thanks for showing me how poor we are, Dad."

God made special, hearty people to live out in the wide open plains—to take life at a little slower pace, even though there is most often more work than a farmer can get done in a day even if he/she never stops; to drive down the dusty country roads in a pickup truck and stop to visit with their neighbor whom they've met on the road. They're sometimes stopped long enough to shut their trucks off as they visit, because nobody else is coming down that road—and probably won't be for a while. And the sky is all around them as they drive around checking fields or checking cows and calves in the pasture, or driving home from their work—which is all around them.

But in choosing for ourselves where to live, the sky really would be the limit. If we couldn't see it, that place would only be seen from our rear view mirrors.

This column by Karen Schwaller first
appeared in *Farm News*.

THE PERILS OF MENDING BLUE JEANS

If only I had been taught this in Home-Ec class. If only I had observed my mother more closely as I was growing up.

Oh, I watched my mother alright—the first farm wife I ever knew, sitting at the sewing machine mending all those jeans through all those years. But at that time in my life, it was HER problem, not mine. What did I care about all the time she spent in front of the sewing machine, mending the jeans that my dad and brothers blew out like a long-lost New Year's Eve party?? I was probably way off, but dare I say that she never seemed to mind doing all that tedious, time-consuming repair work . . . over and over.

Well, let me tell you—it didn't take long after marrying a farmer for me to figure out that I was also going to be doing that same thing. Not only that, but I also don't have the same dutiful demeanor that my mother had while mending jeans.

Mending jeans has been part of my life for the past twenty-five years or so. And mostly what I see are pants with rips comparable to the San Andreas Fault. When the kids notice that one of their siblings has ripped a pair of pants, common phrases like "Mom's gonna be mad!" or "Did you will your stuff to me?" can be heard among them.

And it seems like once you fix them, they should be good to go for a while. Not so at our house. The next time they come through the wash, they're ripped out somewhere else. I swear (and sometimes I do), it's like rabbits. God said to be fruitful and multiply, but I don't think he was talking about ripping out blue jeans at the time. I once had a great aunt who was a housecleaning nun. She served a group of other nuns who apparently were not big on eating potatoes. She once told my mother that when she served three potatoes, she got six back. Oh, if I'd only known how much that is like my mending pile!

This very reason causes me to wonder why I bother to fix farm blue jeans in the first place. I decide at times that if I just leave them on the mending pile then they won't rip out anywhere else, and there will just be that one (albeit very large) hole in the jeans. If I fix them, then I'll just have to fix them again. I could be saving myself a lot of work by just ignoring the whole issue.

Out of curiosity once, I counted the number of patches on a pair of my husband's jeans; I counted thirteen. Naturally, I considered repairing them, but decided that "until death do us part" had finally arrived, and it was time to move them into their next life. Of course, it was a terribly difficult time for me; with all that bonding time together, I felt like we had almost become friends. I nearly had to eulogize them before placing them into the burning barrel.

When our kids were younger, it worked great to leave them on the pile for a while, and then they would outgrow them—leaving me with fewer jeans to fix. Now my husband and I are the ones that outgrow our jeans. Oh, the injustice.

And of course, once you experience the unintentional sewing together of two layers of denim (resulting in 10 minutes of ripping it out and starting again), followed by the accidental dismemberment of a finger due to the combination of a sharp scissors and a few Vodka-Sevens just to get you through it all, you really begin to wonder if it's all worth it.

Yet I know that it is, because as many times as I see jeans on the mending pile, it becomes obvious that we would go broke if I didn't repair them. I just need to do it a little more often, as my family gently nudges me from time to time. They know better than to hound me about it, because my demeanor at the sewing machine is somewhat similar to that of a miniature junk yard dog.

Last week one of my sons said he was completely out of jeans. Of course, I knew he was exaggerating, but he asked me kindly if I could fix a pair of jeans for him before I left for the day. I agreed to do it. He even stood over me—without saying a word—as I fixed them. I broke a needle in the process, and he gratefully thanked me and quickly left the room. That weekend when I finally did get around to fixing all of the jeans that needed repairs, I mended five pair of his jeans alone. I guess he was not exaggerating—and he must feel warmer outside with no leg or fanny flesh greeting the morning air.

That wedding vow of "till death do us part" might just come sooner than we think. I'm just not sure which one of us will part first . . . but be it known that if the jeans go out to the burning barrel sooner, we'll probably both live longer.

My guys have no idea what I contribute to the family fortune.

This column by Karen Schwaller first
appeared in *Farm News*.

WRESTLING WITH THE KIDS

I t's been said that growing old isn't for weenies. That being said, I can attest to that same mantra holding true for being the mother of wrestlers.

Our boys have always been a little on the stocky side—good, strong farm boys who spend most of their summers picking up field rocks and baling in ninety-degree heat, and breaking sheep and calves to lead at the local county 4-H and FFA fair.

So when they entered high school wrestling and started out as freshmen in the varsity arena at the heavyweight level, we all knew it would be quite a ride; but we weren't sure who was going to get the rides. We were glad when freshman year wrestling was over for them. I'm not really into antacids as snacks.

Wrestling is possibly the cruelest sport ever, happening to land directly over the Thanksgiving and Christmas holidays. Whose idea was that anyway? And yet, we know from our boys that it's the only time of year they can even be out for a sport.

The football coaches had salivated for years thinking of those two being on the line. But football season came at the very same time as the harvest, and to them, harvest trumped football, much to the chagrin of the coaches and fans of our school district. Apparently, grain in the grain cart is more of a rush than rushing is.

And so, we progressed into each year with our boys in wrestling. Mothers everywhere know the looks on the faces of other mothers as they watch their sons out on the mat, being twisted and grabbed and thrown down by other wrestlers. It had to have been a sport invented by the male of the species. Our unique ability to experience pregnancy and childbirth automatically counts us out of creating a sport that could allow us to take the chance of our kids getting dropped on their heads and talking like Porky Pig.

On occasion, I've sat mat side and have heard my sons groan in pain when they got taken down ferociously. I've seen them thrown onto their heads, saw one lie on the mat dazed after an especially vigorous throw; watched their arms get twisted until I thought they would snap off; watched their noses bleed, seen black eyes emerge, watched them wrestle guys that weigh 65 pounds more than they do—and win (by the grace of God); and I heard them breathe laboriously as the matches progressed. And I ask you, *why is this fun??*

And yet, we find ourselves mysteriously drawn to this kind of modern-day cock-fighting, and find ourselves really getting into it—even daring to go home hoarse from all that encouraging and coaching we do from the stands.

How could God make mothers like this? I wondered with each event if I would give myself a reason to go to confession the next day.

A mother recently told me that it's really fun to watch your kids wrestle when they are winning, and I can attest to the truthfulness of that statement. Our boys had a couple of tremendous seasons in their junior and senior years.

As hard as it is to watch your kids get tossed around like that by guys who are much more rhinoceros-like than they, it's still exciting. I sit near a friend who becomes very animated as her son wrestles.

Her excitement is great exercise for me as well, making sure my ear plugs are in securely, ducking her flailing arms and leaning away from her upper cut as she shouts praise, encouragement, and coaches her son from the stands. For me and others around her, it's much the same as training for a plane crash—covering the head, leaning forward and hoping for the best.

But for our family, wrestling is where it's at. In defense of the sport, it's much warmer to sit and watch than football. I'm not a fan of frostbite and wearing snowmobile suits at a sporting event unless I'm in Norway watching the winter Olympics.

Thinking back, I remember when people in our community were really wanting our boys to go out for youth football when they were in fourth or fifth grade. It was ridiculously expensive to do for one child, let alone two kids, so we opted to not do it. After all, times weren't that great on the farm. But when questioned about it once by a mother whose son, Brady (who was much smaller in size than our boys) was really into it, I told her, "Well, I'm afraid they'll get hurt." (It was only a small lie. I was well aware of their man-sized clumsiness ever since they were first toddling around, even knocking over our Christmas tree once while they were still in diapers.)

I'll always remember her reply. She said, "You're worried that your boys will get hurt? What if one of your boys falls on my Brady?"

Wow. I truly hadn't thought about it that way.

This column by Karen Schwaller first
appeared in *Farm News*.

THOUGHTS ON GETTING OLDER

Maybe it's a thing that comes with age. Or perhaps, one of the *many* things that come with it.

When we were young and on the farm, we learned that the area that we would otherwise call a cows' neck, is the "brisket," not the "basket." (Cow Anatomy 101: it comes right after "Barn Etiquette vs. Table Manners.")

And when we get a little older, we learn that chickens and baby chicks have stomachs that are so small, that they eat all the time. Nowhere in the "Chicken Analysis 101" section did it say that humans should adapt that exquisite dining philosophy, but of course, I've always thought that what's good for the goose is good for the gander . . . er, wait . . . what's good for the chicken is good for . . . well, never mind that one.

We also learn that it's difficult to ride a pig, to get your boot out of knee-deep manure without losing your balance and stepping stocking-footed into the manure; to keep playing cards stiff over and over again when you use them to make your two-wheeler sound like a motorcycle, to walk to the house with frozen winter clothes after you've fallen through the ice of the nearby creek, and to fit into a canner tub when you live 10 or 15 miles from the nearest swimming pool. Aah, those were the days.

Then we fast-forward a few years to when we have kids of our own, and they learn all of those things as we watch. Oh, the glory of being older and wiser! But one thing I didn't think about as I was growing up was that I would be learning things for the rest of my life. Not that I've always *wanted* to learn things, but it's a necessary reality of this life.

I have learned not to be surprised when, during the week before our county fair, I open the cupboard under the sink and reach for the dish soap, and end up with a handful of cobwebs instead. Naturally, the dish soap is outside where they are washing cows and sheep . . . don't all housewives keep their dish soap supply outside in the cattle barn???

I have found lately that age spots have crept into my existence. As I was applying make-up the other day, I realized with great horror that I could qualify for the speckle-faced sheep class at our 4-H and FFA fair sheep show. If I walked on my hands and knees and glued on a tail, no one would know the difference. And with four legs and a tail, my very busy farmer guys might actually take note that I'm here this time of year!

But there are also all those other things that come with it . . . like our ability (or lack thereof) to shed a few pounds. My pounds tend to "go into the shed" instead, to stay. Thank God I tend to carry around some spare change in my purse, because when I make a purchase and give it to the cashier, it's the only way I feel like I can lose weight. At least my purse feels lighter, and that has to count for something.

Then there's that whole memory loss thing . . . who invented that, anyway? And when I can't read what's right in front of me, I recall the words of my mother as I was growing up, who (I now realize) was the woman with the golden tongue. She always told me, "You can't see past the end of your nose." She was probably a fortune teller in a previous life.

But it's really so aggravating when all of these things work together to make your life miserable. Recently I decided I needed a larger purse because I always had things hanging out of the one I was carrying. It was looking frumpy and most unfashionable— and didn't do well for my look of professional office clothes that I could wear to work, or to chase sheep in when they get out of the pasture during office hours. My new purse needed to be part purse, part disguiser of my half-century-aged body, and part briefcase because I tend to carry some paper work back and forth between home and work. It's an office on straps; almost Clay County Fair-like, and a middle-aged woman's dream.

A couple of weeks ago I placed something in there to mail when I got to town, then promptly forgot about it. It was like I had placed that envelope in a black hole. Thank God I needed to add to my grocery list the following week, and saw that envelope which should have been mailed the week before. As I stood there making up excuses about what I was going to tell those people, it occurred to me that a large purse and a short memory are not a good combination.

At least I didn't misplace a kid in there anywhere or find Jimmy Hoffa . . . or even my long-lost sanity. That would probably have put me over the edge. But who knows? Maybe I'd like it over there.

This column by Karen Schwaller first
appeared in *Farm News*.

ABOUT THE AUTHOR

Karen Schwaller lives in Milford, Iowa with her husband on their family farm. Their three children are grown—proud products of the family farm, and proud to all be working in agriculture. She has been a writer and photographer all of her adult life, writing news, human-interest stories and columns for various publications in northwest Iowa, on both a full-time and freelance basis.

She spent fourteen years directing her parish religious education program in the middle of it, which gave her a new perspective from which to write as a result of her deepened faith. From that experience, she gained a new understanding that farmers work hand-in-hand with God to provide for their families and feed the world. She especially enjoys writing about farm life and rural living, and all of the things (happy or sad) that happen on the family farm. She herself is a product of a family farm near Remsen, Iowa.

Made in the USA
Middletown, DE
01 November 2022